SUFISM, ISLAM AND JUNGIAN PSYCHOLOGY

Other Titles in the Jungian Series
By J. Marvin Spiegelman

Catholicism and Jungian Psychology
Buddhism and Jungian Psychology
Hinduism and Jungian Psychology
Judaism and Jungian Psychology: A Modern Jew in Search
    of a Soul
Protestantism and Jungian Psychology
Sufism , Islam and Jungian Psychology
The Tree
The Knight
The Quest
The Nymphomaniac
Jungian Analysts: Their Visions and Vulnerabilities
Jungian Psychology and the Passions of the Soul
The Unhealed Healer: Reich, Jung, Regardie and Me
The Unpublished Writer: Rider Haggard, Henry Miller and
    Me

And to get your free catalog of all of our titles, write to:

New Falcon Publications
Catalog Dept.
7025 East 1st Avenue #5
Scottsdale, AZ 85257 U.S.A.

SUFISM, ISLAM AND JUNGIAN PSYCHOLOGY

EDITED BY

J. MARVIN SPIEGELMAN, PH.D.

WITH

PIR VILAYAT INAYAT KHAN

AND

TASNIM FERNANDEZ

1991
NEW FALCON PUBLICATIONS
(FALCON PRESS)
SCOTTSDALE, ARIZONA U.S.A.

International Standard Book Number: 1-56184-015-7

First Edition 1991

NEW FALCON PUBLICATIONS
7025 East 1st Avenue #5
Scottsdale, AZ 85257 U.S.A.
(602) 246-3546

TABLE OF CONTENTS

Introduction

"I dreamt that I was in an Arab city, and as in most such cities there was a citadel, a casbah. The city was situated in a broad plain, and had a wall around it. The shape of the wall was square, and there were four gates.

"The casbah in the interior of the city was surrounded by a wide moat (which is not the way it really is in Arab countries).

"I stood before a wooden bridge leading over the water to a dark, horseshoe-shaped portal, which was open. Eager to see the citadel from the inside also, I stepped out on the bridge. When I was about halfway across it, a handsome, dark Arab of aristocratic, almost royal bearing came toward me from the gate. I knew that this youth in the white burnoose was the resident prince of the citadel. When he came up to me, he attacked me and tried to knock me down. We wrestled. In the struggle we crashed against the railing; it gave way and both of us fell into the moat, where he tried to push my head under water to drown me. No, I thought, this is going too far. And in my turn I pushed his head under water. I felt great admiration for him; but I did not want to let myself be killed. I had no intention of killing him; I wanted only to make him unconscious and incapable of fighting.

"Then the scene of the dream changed, and he was with me in a large vaulted octagonal room in the center of the citadel. The room was all white, very plain and beautiful. Along the light-colored marble walls stood low divans, and before me on the floor lay an open book with black letters written in magnificent calligraphy on milky-white parchment. It was not Arabic script; rather, it looked to me like the Vigurian script of West Turkestan, which was familiar to me from the Manichaean fragments from Turfan. I did not know the contents, but nevertheless I had the feeling that this was 'my book,' that I had written it. The young prince with whom I had just been wrestling sat to the right of me on the floor. I explained to him that now that I had overcome him he must read the book. But he resisted. I placed my arm around his shoulders and forced him, with a sort of paternal kindness and patience, to read the book. I knew that this was absolutely essential, and at last he yielded." (C.G. Jung's dream in North Africa, in 1920, in *Memories*, pp. 242-243)

Jung's religious attitude, despite his natal Christianity, was directed toward the psyche. So focussed, he reached out — or better said, he reached in — toward other religions since they draw their symbolism from those deep strata of the soul which speak to common experiences of the divine and which Jung discovered in his work with his own dreams and those of patients. His autobiographical *Memories* attests to this inner connection as does his remarkable scholarship, evidenced throughout his work. All of the world religions, as well as many of the local variants of animistic worship, are referred to by him. His work has impacted Zoroastrians and Taoists, as well as those from the more familiar denominations, east and west. Our ongoing series of books on Jungian psychology and the religions give some record of this (see overleaf).

Jung's relation to Islam, however, is somewhat mysterious. That he was deeply immersed in Arabic alchemy is readily apparent in many of his volumes which demonstrate the parallels between the ancient arcane art and the modern discovery of individuation. We learn by indirection that he was at least reasonably familiar with the Quran, sufficiently so for one Somali man brought up in the Sufi faith to refer to Jung as a "man of the Book" ("Concerning Rebirth" in Vol. 9, part I, p. 143). In that same essay, he discourses knowledgeably and at length on Khidr, a figure who plays a great role in Islamic mysticism. (More about Khidr later on). Yet he wrote no essays on Islam or Sufism themselves, rather surprising when we consider his informed and appreciative works on aspects of Buddhism and Hinduism, as well as Christianity. His great ecumenical dreams and experiences of his old age, including Judaism, Greek polytheism and Christianity (*Memories*, pp. 293-295), the basis of the western psyche, notably did not include a Muslim image. It is likely, as I note in my essay on active imagination in this book, that the works of some Islamic mystics such as Ibn 'Arabi (as well as Jewish mystics) were available to him only very late in life. But the dreams and hints having to do with Islam and Sufism in his autobiographical memoirs, including the one given at the outset of this introduction, are thought-provoking and worthy of consideration here.

Before we take those up, however, it is important to note that although no Islamic scholar, to my knowledge, has involved himself with Jungian psychology the way those of the other faiths have (including undergoing analysis and even becoming qualified in that field), Jung was sufficiently well thought of in Moslem circles to have been given an honorary doctorate at the Islamic university in

Allahabad, along with Hindu and scientific recognition from other universities, when he was in India. There is mystery enough here, one thinks, for fuller investigation some time. My inquiries as to Jung's connection with these matters were not productive, so we are left with the record, notably the *Memories*, which we will now consider.

The first mention of things Arabic or Islamic occurs in the chapter on his student years. We suddenly learn that Jung's father — who has previously been presented as a rather kindly but not very intellectual country pastor of the Swiss Reformed Church — received a Ph.D. in oriental languages and did his dissertation on an Arabic version of the Song of Songs of Solomon! Until this point, we were led to believe that the senior Jung could not help the junior because of both his religious doubts and lack of understanding of such conundrums as the Trinity. We are, therefore, in no way prepared for a simple Protestant minister to be so knowledgeable in oriental languages and Arabic! Sure enough, we learn later on that the senior Jung probably had initial talents and capacities which failed to be developed and which, perhaps, contributed to his lamentable depression, but surely a person who has learned enough to do a dissertation on the Arabic version of the Song of Songs has both the intellect and passion to be a suitable father for the person who might be considered a leading figure of twentieth century psychology and religion! So somehow that interest and capacity was in the background for the youthful C.G. Jung and that aspect of his father's spirit and talent must have impacted him in unknown ways, despite the junior Jung's tremendous religious precocity and independence.

The next mention of Islamic matters occurs in his chapter on The Work, where he reports his big dream of being unable to submit totally ("For some reason I could not bring my forehead quite down to the floor — there was perhaps a millimeter to spare", *Memories* , p. 219). In this "big dream," there is mention of a large hall, which was an exact replica of the divan-i-kaas (council hall) of the Sultan Akbar at Fatehpur Sikri. This gigantic mandala was a center for a hero figure, like David and Alexander, who could rule over large areas of "this world." From it, as a basis, one could ascend to higher, spiritual realization, which occurs later in the dream. Notably, Jung's father appears in this dream, as a custodian of sarcophagi belonging to famous people, and also as an interpreter of the Pentateuch who speaks with such swiftness and profundity as to make the several psychiatrists present unable to understand him. Jung rightly interpreted these doctors as parts of his shadow, but we might also see here the correction provided by the unconscious for Jung's perhaps insufficient appreciation of his father's capacity. (Aspects of this dream are discussed by Father Doran and also by me in the book, *Catholicism and Jungian Psychology*).

A fuller presentation of Jung's understanding of Arab culture and mentality is given by the eight-page description of his experiences while travelling in North Africa (*Memories*, pp. 238-246). He was haunted by the "blood" of many battles and several civilizations on this Moorish land, and touched by the emotional intensity he sensed among the people, in contrast with Europeans. The male-dominated culture and emotional closeness among them reminded him of ancient Greece and he sensed the absence of the frenetic, watch-dominated consciousness from which he came. Stirred by the atmosphere, the invocation of the muezzin at dawn, the impact of witnessing the profound effect of a holy man among the people, all made him realize that he had, indeed, fallen under the spell of this land. He then had the dream we reported at the outset.

Jung's interpretation of this dream is quite instructive. He recognized the Arab youth — a double of a proud Arab who had ridden past him without greeting during the day — as a figuration of the Self, or rather, an emissary of the Self, since he emerged out of the perfect mandala of the citadel. We might also note here that Jung's dream of the divan-i-kaas also made use of the mandala imagery. The struggle with this figure is similar to the motif of Jacob's struggle with the angel, "the messenger of God who wished to kill men because he did not know them." Jung felt that this "angel" should have dwelt within him, but that both had to learn from each other before this could take place.

Jung remarks that his encounter with Arab culture had struck him overwhelmingly, that the emotional nature of the people, much closer to life than he, touched historical layers within him which helped him to gain some perspective on his own European condition. The Arab was seen as a shadow, but not a personal one; "As master of the casbah, he must be regarded as a kind of shadow of the self."

That Jung was struck by the more emotional, "primitive" aspects of his surroundings was not a negative event nor even unique (he experienced something similar in black Africa). It was a pity, however, that he did not also encounter more differentiated Islamic personalities or become aware of aspects of the religion that were revealed to him toward the end of his life at the Eranos meetings, such as the lectures of the great French Islamicist, Henri Corbin.

Jung's dream, however, says much to us about our collective condition at this time of cultural and religious interpenetration, barely begun during his visit to the Sahara in 1920. It seems very true that Arab and Islamic consciousness is an aspect of the Self which is still quite "in the dark" for European/American consciousness and that the outer events over the last couple of decades is symbolic of that mutual lack of connection.

Could it be that Jung knew unconsciously that it would be of great value if that "other side" could also be aware of his work, particularly in its syncretic character, and based on elements (the Mithraic text) which preceded the separation of the three great western religions? I think that this may not only be possible, but even necessary, if the "Middle East" can carry out its "bridging" function between east and west. The bridge of Jung's dream is a worthy symbol of this place of meeting. One hopes that such connections can now begin to be made.

A further insight into this dream was provided me by Dr. Sonja Marjasch of Zurich. She referred me to a book by Peter Hopkirk called *Foreign Devils on the Silk Road* where we are informed that the discoverer of Manichaean manuscripts and wall paintings was one Albert von Le Coq, an adventurous archaeologist who was active during the same period as Jung's dream. Rather startlingly, a photograph is presented of Le Coq (p.69) who looks astoundingly like Jung himself! Dr. Marjasch was also struck by the likeness and marvelled at the fact that while Jung was undertaking his inner journey of discovery, Le Coq and the other archaeologists were making the outer ones. Synchronicity, perhaps?

One needs to say a bit more about Manichaeism and the texts mentioned in the dream. The religion was born in Persia during the 3rd century, and was based on two opposing principles, Light (the spirit) and Darkness (the flesh). Its founder, Manes (whose portrait was found by Le Coq), and his disciples, were ruthlessly persecuted by the Christians in the West. At the end of the fifth century, they went eastward to Chinese Central Asia. Hopkirk informs us (p. 27) that "until the German archaeologists began to unearth whole Manichaean libraries in the Turfan region, this creed appeared to have no literature and was known chiefly by the violently hostile writings of its opponents, notably St. Augustine." The Uighur Turks converted to this religion in the eighth century and it enjoyed a period of growth and acceptance until it was violently supplanted by the "tidal wave of Islam." We can see, with Sonja Marjasch, how Jung, with his interest in the opposites, could be compelling the Arab prince to read the book in

Uighur script. I should think that he is trying to both influence the Self of the west with its powerfully monotheistic aspect, yet also wanting to be connected to it. His dream, still pregnant with meaning, awaits further interpretation. In his other remarks, Jung wonders what the technological age will do with Islam. In our present day, we may also ask what Islam may do with technology! It is of great importance, I think, that the mutual withdrawal of the projections of the dark side (the Great Satan) take place and be facilitated. That is surely one of the aims of the present volume.

In this connection, we can say something more about Jung's contact with the more developed aspects of Arabic and Islamic culture. This is perhaps best accomplished when we look at his treatment of the Khidr legend.

In his essay, "Concerning Rebirth" (Vol. 9, i, pp. 11-147), Jung uses the figure of Khidr and the 18th Sura of the Quran for "a typical set of symbols illustrating the process of transformation (pp. 135-147)." Taking place in "The Cave," suggests it as a rebirth mystery. Jung interprets the entire text with both mastery and sympathy but with a judgment about which I have a small cavil, mentioned at the end of this introduction. The cave itself and the legend of the Seven Sleepers who remain there for 309 years is understood by Jung to signify that anyone who finds himself in the darkness of the unconscious will undergo a process of transformation, a momentous change of personality in either a positive or negative sense, grasped sometimes as a prolongation of life or hint of immortality, as it is also expressed in alchemy. "The fate of the numinous figures," says Jung, "grips the hearer, because the story gives expression to parallel processes in his own unconscious which in that way are integrated into consciousness again. The repristination of the original state is tantamount to attaining once more the freshness of youth."

The story of the sleepers is followed by some moral observations which, as Jung points out, have no connection with the text. Here Jung makes some pithy remarks about experience and religious rules of behavior which may be offensive to those who follow the normative pattern (p. 236-7):

> In reality, these edifying comments are just what are needed by those who cannot be reborn themselves and have to be contented with moral conduct, that is to say with adherence to the law. Very often behavior prescribed by rule is a substitute for spiritual transformation.

In a footnote, Jung gives parallel examples from St. Paul, who distinguishes between the spiritual man (pneumatikos) and the carnal man (sarkikos), the latter of which must conform to the law, while the former can become free. Yet both principles can be found in the same person, of course. Jung's view is that the Quran text says, in effect, that the legend promises rebirth to those who have ears to hear, but that those who do not will "find satisfaction and safe guidance in blind submission to Allah's will."

This has been a typical understanding within Jungian circles in the past and no doubt there are many examples to confirm it. I can recall hearing a senior and respected faculty member at the C.G. Jung Institute in Zurich complain that a particular Eastern person was not yet ready to become an analyst since he was "too much contained in his religion." What she meant, of course, was the danger that one did not have the religious experience directly and individually, but all was filtered through the revealed and established patterns.

Since those days, however, there are not a few individuals who have remained within the structure of their faith, advanced their individuation and even become Jungian analysts (e.g. Catholic priests). One must distinguish, therefore, between individuation and individualism. Just as the latter in no way betokens spiritual freedom and particularity, the former is not confined to apostates. I recall a lecture of Professor Zwi Werblowsky of Hebrew University who pointed out that many of the greatest figures in Jewish mysticism, such as Caro and Luria, also admonished careful observance of the law, and that the two are not necessarily mutually exclusive. This is also true, as I understand it, for such a profound Islamic figure as Ibn 'Arabi (see paper on active imagination). Yet he, too, recognizes a difference between personal dialogue with the divine and what is revealed "in the faiths."

Jung continues his interpretation by recounting the Quranic story of Moses, who represents the individual on a quest for transformation, together with his servant "shadow," Joshua ben Nun. They encounter Khidr as a teacher and undergo surprising, even startlingly immoral, experiences with him. Moses learns, however, the greater wisdom of his teacher, who appears at the Isthmus of Suez, where the Eastern and Western seas come close together, the "place of the middle" mentioned earlier. "They had forgotten their fish, the humble source of nourishment, who refers to Nun, the father of the shadow, the carnal man, who comes from the dark world of the Creator." The fish is a symbol of a content of the instinctive unconscious, a source of renewal found in the condition of "loss of soul," such as being hungry or "worn out," one known to us all. The typical motif of "failure to recognize a moment of crucial importance" is noted here, as is the hint of finding the source of life and then losing it again, a theme also known in alchemy and expanded upon in the Quranic commentaries.

Jung shows how the fish is a prefiguration of Khidr, who is understood by him as a symbol of the Self, having been born in a cave, is the "Long-lived One," continually renews himself like Elijah, and is also his friend. Khidr is accepted as a higher consciousness although the tale is alarming. Jung tells us that this is how ego-consciousness reacts to the superior guidance of the Self through the twists and turns of fate:

> To the initiate who is capable of transformation it is a comforting tale; to the obedient believer, an exhortation to not murmur against Allah's incomprehensible omnipotence. Khidr symbolizes not only the higher wisdom but also a way of acting which is in accord with this wisdom and transcends reason.

We are all the questing Moses, says Jung, and what is transformed, he notes, is neither Moses nor Joshua, but the forgotten fish. It begins in a humble place and undergoes the hero's myth. It is the higher personality within us, the Self, which undergoes transformation, Jung shows, with parallels in other religions. Our intuition of immortality refers to the non-spatial and non-temporal aspects of ourselves, and Khidr is that aspect of the Self which is revealed as a personality who so survives and transforms.

Jung remarks that Khidr lives on, in the religion of the people, as friend, adviser, comforter and teacher of revealed wisdom.

Khidr's character as a friend is shown in the subsequent part of the Eighteenth Sura, wherein the figure of Dhulqarnein, the Two-Horned One, (Alexander the Great), is brought in, with the "lack of coherence" often found in Mohammed's chronology. Jung explains the discrepancy from a psychological point-of-view:

> Moses had a profoundly moving experience of the self, which brought unconscious processes before his eyes with overwhelming clarity. Afterwards, when he comes to his people, the Jews, who are counted among the infidels, and wants to tell them about his experience, he prefers to use the form of a mystery legend. Instead of speaking about himself, he speaks about the Two-Horned One. Since Moses himself is also "horned," the substitution of Dhulqarnein appears plausible.

What Jung means here is that the impersonal mystery legend is given as a transformation happening to the "other." "Although it is Moses himself who, in his experience with Khidr, stands in Dhulqarnein's place, he has to name the latter instead of himself in telling the story." Jung understands this as a way to avoid inflation, the great psychic danger when one encounters the Self. He shows that the Quran makes no distinction between Khidr and Allah, indicating that the former is an "incarnation," so to speak, of the latter. We also note that the theme of the pair of friends is recurrent and Jung makes a non-flattering parallel with the German psyche in the Faust story. The two-fold aspect of the Self, we might say, is a representation of its attempt to ensure its survival in "the place of the middle" (e.g. Jerusalem), when threatened by envious collective forces. Its psychological meaning, says Jung, is that individuation is an *opus contra naturam*, which can collapse under such collective impact and return to an initial state of opposites untransformed, in contrast to the needed and hoped-for union of them, the *complexio oppositorum*.

Jung concludes this interpretation of the Eighteenth Sura as follows:

> In spite of its apparently disconnected and allusive character, it (the Sura) gives an almost perfect picture of a psychic transformation or rebirth which today, with our greater psychological insight, we would recognize as an individuation process. Because of the great age of the legend and the Islamic prophet's primitive cast of mind, the process takes place entirely outside the sphere of consciousness and is projected in the form of a mystery legend or a pair of friends and the deeds they perform. That is why it is all so allusive and lacking in logical sequence. Nevertheless, the legend expresses the obscure archetype of transformation so admirably that the passionate religious eros of the Arab finds it completely satisfying. It is for this reason that the figure of Khidr plays such an important part in Islamic mysticism.

What are we to make of this somewhat ambivalent presentation of Jung's understanding of a crucial text in Islamic scripture? First of all, it is brilliant and helpful and appreciative, but an Islamic believer will not take kindly to the "primitive cast of mind" attributed to the Prophet, any more than Jews would take kindly to their religious leader being seen, in the Quran, as a somewhat foolish person who must find the light from a subsequent Prophet who has transcended him and his people's wisdom.

I think that we are dealing here with a frequent shadow problem involving any growth of consciousness and magnified when we confront it at a collective level: the previous height of awareness needs to be denigrated somehow. It is as if one's parents must be defeated and made "less-than" so that we can find and enjoy our own individuality. If we pursue this analogy with human growth, however, the adolescent ultimately grows up and appreciates the values of his parents without having to denigrate them. This is less customary in religious development, alas, as we know from our religious wars and texts. Yet it may be the particular task and achievement of our own and the coming decades to arrive at that desired position of "appreciation" of the various paths to the divine, affirmation of one's own and one's tribe's truths, without having to destroy or be superior to the other languages of God. Perhaps we can even develop sufficiently to perform comparisons in the field of psychology and religion, indicating where one formulation may be, indeed, superior to others in that particular aspect, without having to arrive at the false conclusion that one religion is better than another. Perhaps that is one useful function of the psychological approach itself, as long as it does not, in turn, arrogate to itself a position of superiority!

Jung originally presented his lecture on rebirth at the Eranos conference in 1938, before his great ecumenical dreams and before he became acquainted with more knowledgeable theologians and scholars in Islam and Judaism. The later Jung, for example, understood the worldly versus other-worldly aspects of the Self as shown in Dhulqarnein and Khidr, (as shown in his commentary on his dream with the divan-i-kaas) but did not write much about it. It remains for others to continue the task of psychological reflection and comparison of the religious themes and experiences which Jung began and which is so richly described in all his astounding volumes. Our present book is a small venture on this path; we hope that others will continue.

The various contributors to our volume, although small in number, constitute a valuable nucleus of quite diverse people, sharing a great appreciation of both Jungian psychology and Islam, particularly Sufism.

Tasnim Fernandez was graciously helpful in arranging for the contributions by members of the Sufi Order. I am particularly grateful for the papers of Pir Vilayat Inayat Khan and Professor Mohammed Shaalan, both of whom come from long and profound Islamic traditions and have reached out in a rich ecumenical fashion. The former, of course, is world-famed as a leader in modern Sufism and the latter is an illustrious professor of psychiatry in Egypt. May their — and our — appreciative reflections find receptive minds for further development of our common spiritual aims.

A further word needs to be said about the two Sufi organizations that are represented in this book — indeed, all the contributors except Shaalan and Spiegelman are members of them. The Sufi Order, headed by Pir Vilayat Inayat Khan, was founded by his father, Hazrat Inayat Khan in 1910, of the lineage of the Chisti Order, Ajmer, India, who was the first to introduce Sufism in the West. Pir Vilayat resides in Paris but travels widely and the headquarters of his organization is in Seattle, Washington. This Order has the mission "to spread the message of unity and promote the awakening of humanity to the divinity in all... To provide a program of spiritual training to bring about a deep personal transformation... To develop spiritual guides... To find new ways to apply the spiritual ideals of love, harmony, and beauty... To serve God and humanity..." To accomplish this they have an Esoteric School, Retreats, School of the Universal Worship, a Healing Order, as well as a publishing house and home study courses. The following contributors to the present volume are members of this Order: Tasnim Fernandez, Atum O'Kane, Don Weiner, and Pir Vilayat Inayat Khan.

Our second Sufi group is headed by Irina Tweedie, who was initiated and trained by her Guru in India according to the Naqshbandi line. This group is headquartered in England, with participating contributors for this volume including Brigitte Dorst, LLewellyn Vaughan-Lee, as well as Irina Tweedie.

Mohammed Shaalan describes his own Sufi experience in his article.

The undersigned wants to express his appreciation for the assistance and good will expressed by both of these organizations and their members who freely gave of themselves for this project.

> J. Marvin Spiegelman
> Studio City, California
> April 1989; Ramadan 1409

References

Hopkirk, Peter, FOREIGN DEVILS ON THE SILK ROAD: The search for the Lost Cities and Treasures or Chinese Central Asia, John Murray (Publishers) Ltd., London, 1980. 252 pp.

Jung, C.G., MEMORIES, DREAMS, REFLECTIONS, Pantheon, New York, 1961.

Jung, C.G., "Concerning Rebirth", in Vol. 9, Part I, of COLLECTED WORKS.

The Master, The Student and The Sufi-group: Sufi-Relationships Today

By Birgitte Dorst

Sufism and Analytical Psychology

To write and to read about Sufism and Analytical Psychology is like being involved with a cookbook. There are recipes that look very attractive, but what the dishes actually will taste like, nobody will ever experience by studying cookbooks.

So reading a text like this one will only point to the possibilities of experience, just as recipes will only show up possibilities of preparing a dish. And a Sufi needs to be cooked for a long time until he or she is well done.

Of course this is not only true to the essence of Sufism but of Analytical Psychology as well. Nobody will understand anything of what the process of individuation means who has not realized some steps.

Archetypes remain vague concepts unless their operating power and their influence has not been experienced in your own dreams, images, imaginations and the events of your daily life.

Talking about the relations between Sufism and modern Western Psychology, Idries Shah comments:

> "Sufism itself is a much more advanced psychological system than all systems developed so far in the Occidental world. This psychology in its essence is not Eastern but Human." (1981, p.54)

Very much along these lines, C.G. Jung makes the point that Western psychology compared to its Eastern equivalents has not gone beyond its very initial phases.

> "What we consider to be a specifically Occidental invention, that is to say psychoanalysis and all the impulses taken their origin in it, is only a beginner's attempt, when compared to ancient traditional art." (*Collected Works*, 10, p.109)

19

In Sufism and in Analytical Psychology the central issue is development of awareness and consciousness, leading the human person from a state of unawareness to levels of higher consciousness. In both models the path is regarded as a process of transformation towards the Self.

For analytical work one needs two elements, the analyst and the analysand. Sufism on the other hand essentially requires three elements, the teacher, the student and the spiritual community, the Sufi group.

In the analytical model the analysand chooses his analyst, in the Sufi context the attraction comes from the teacher. It is the teacher who attracts the student as soon as the student is ready.

The work done by analyst and analysand is mysterious in its nature and difficult to explain. C.G. Jung refers to the alchemical image of the 'vas hermeticum', in which both are locked up and transformed. The process happens on the psychological levels and within the boundaries of time and space.

Part of the transformation process experienced by the Sufi-student happens beyond the boundaries of time and space, leading into mystical experience, which cannot be conveyed with words.

For many students it is quite difficult to find a clear orientation within Analytical Psychology. Searching through the Collected Works of C.G. Jung for a logical structure and a well-ordered system is doomed to failure.

Sufism is even more a systemless system, which changes its momentary Gestalt constantly and adapts itself to the requirements of the moment.

Rules, rites and concepts are forms, just like clothes, which also have undergone constant change in the course of the centuries. Just like many elements of the theories of Jung have become common knowledge, traces of Sufism can be found in the history, arts and wisdom teaching of many peoples and many countries: in the Jewish Cabbala, in European philosophy, in Arab stories and poems, in medieval architecture, for instance the cathedrals in Europe, in Hinduism as well as in Christian mysticism.

In his book *The Sufis* (1981) I. Shah describes these connections.

Nevertheless, Sufism transcends Philosophy, Arts, Religions and Psychology altogether.

What Sufism is NOT

It is comparatively easy to name the most important elements of Jungian Psychology: the concept of individuation, the conscious and the unconscious, ego and self, personal and collective unconscious, the theory of archetypes, the approaches to the human psyche as conceived by depth psychology using dreams, images, symbols, imagination, fairy-tales and myths.

What Sufism is in its essence cannot be defined clearly and can only be understood in the context of a Sufi training.

It is much easier to say what Sufism is not:

It is not mysterious wisdom, not the esoteric aspect of Islam, it is not a body of teaching, it is not a religious system, not a secret order of Arab men, not magic, not mysticism or tradition and yet any of these areas may contain seeds of Sufism. Sufism is not a teaching or a movement that can be pinned down to a special time or local area.

"Sufism is truth without form" (Irina Tweedie).

Like Zen it is non-teaching.

Sufism is a kind of yeast which triggers fermentation processes in the psyche. We could say it is the yeast in the process of evolution, promoting the awakening of mankind.

Not teaching, nor tradition, but time and social conditions determine the momentary living Gestalt of Sufism.

Contemporary Sufism uses present-day teaching and learning methods, taking into account the political, social, emotional and intellectual conditions of modern life.

Contemporary Sufis are very ordinary people, their lifestyle is in no way different from the lifestyle in their environment; they are quite normal people.

The Teacher

In Sufism a teacher is an absolute necessity, and this is elucidated by the following example:

In order to heat water to the right degree, a mediator is needed, a pot between water and fire.

The Sufi teacher fulfills the role of this mediator and yet has no claim to be personally important.

In Sufism it is said: the teacher is without name.

He or she doesn't work through teaching but through being. The teacher is an energetic current. The student, who submerges himself into it, is influenced by these energetic forces and his process is speeded up.

When I met my teacher for the first time, a flash went through me and a thought: "Never before in my life have I met a human being radiating so much love!"

The presence of the master or a real teacher is therefore an indescribable joy and sometimes a fear, at the same time giving rise to a deep longing to reach the source of this love oneself. The presence of the teacher is a nourishing spiritual motherliness, supporting the students in their growth.

For that purpose it is necessary to be together, not in communication but in communion, allowing a current to go from heart to heart. It is difficult to describe this form of being together, the Indians have a special word for it: Satsang.

It is easier to describe how the teacher deals with the student in the initial phases. There are similarities to what the analyst does with his analysand; he assesses the level of development, he diagnoses the student's present difficulties and problems, daily life problems as well as spiritual problems and starts the work at this very point.

Part of the work is the interpretation of dreams, which mirror the inner state of the student and his level of spiritual advancement.

Dreams and all soul experiences during the night are essential on the Sufi path. Many a teaching or advice is given by indirect confrontation. Thus the teacher may talk to somebody about a certain issue. But what he says is not only for that person, and by intuition you happen to know it's a message for you.

It is up to the teacher to remove the rust and all the covers which obstruct the consciousness of the student. Thus his task is one of purifying, clarifying and destroying obstacles.

The behavior of a real teacher is unpredictable. It comes unexpectedly and plays with the whole variety of human behavior. Not all the students gathering around the teacher are treated in the same way; on the contrary, the master treats them very differently in accordance with their needs.

You may recognize a genuine master by the fact that he or she treats every person individually.

Bad teachers behave according to the expectations of their followers.

To be a master means to be capable of recognizing what a person needs in that very moment, to take the responsibility, that is to have the right response in what he says, does or reflects.

"A Saint has no desires, he never indulges in anything because he becomes universal, belonging to the people. It is a law that what can be done by simple means should be so done;

no spiritual power should be wasted. One must never waste spiritual Energy. No two Shishyas (students) are treated alike; human beings are unique, and the Guru, if he is a Sat Guru and knows his job, will treat them according to their possibilities, their character, and past conditioning." (Tweedie, 1986, p. 141)

A Sufi teacher is an energy channel, a link between the student and the goal. Both are united in a loving relationship, which is timeless and entirely different from the analytical relationship limited by time and roles.

A Sufi teacher directs the student in such a way that he will attain knowledge and understanding through his own effort and his own experience and development. In this aspect he is similar to the analyst. Sufi literature, therefore, describes the teacher, sometimes, as a doctor or the healer who is able to cure diseases and weaknesses of the human soul. He reads the student's mind, diagnoses and observes the movements of the conscious and the unconscious, gives attention to dreams and all inner experiences and helps to understand them.

Hints and recommendations for spiritual development in a hidden or allegorical way are to be found in many Sufi stories and proverbs.

The student understands according to his level.

Sufi stories are like onions with many different layers.

The Student

The relationship between teacher and student can only be described paradoxically. The student remains entirely free; he or she never submits to the teacher but can only advance on the path to the extent that he or she surrenders to the power of the teacher or the Guru principle. (Gu-ru means from dark [gu] to light [ru]).

This surrender is a second birth, becoming the one who I really am.

At the same time it is a process of becoming released from the ego, in Jungian terms from the conditioning attached to the personal and focussing in the ego and not in the self.

To become a Sufi is a process of spiritual intuition (tuition from within), in-sight and growth.

There is nothing to gain, no academic knowledge, no prestige but many things to lose: self-concepts and self-images, personal convictions and opinions, personal values, the products of education and family heritage, in short all the conditioning and everything that binds to the past.

The Sufi path starts where the person begins to recognize that so far he or she understands nothing, that there is only confusion. Depending on the degree of disturbances, conditioning and handicaps, analytical work is needed and helpful. Therefore it may be quite possible that the Sufi Master recommends to students some analytical or therapeutic work, especially in the beginning.

In our group, several students do this.

On the other hand quite a few members of the group are well-trained therapists of different schools.

However, the background of Sufi students may be very different. The members of our group in London represent a very mixed community, bringing together people of the most varied jobs, degrees of education, social status, colour, age and nationality. Women are the majority, but it doesn't really matter if you are a British housewife, a German professor or an Italian pizza-baker. And even time doesn't matter. Some members live in London, others come from time to time from any place in the world for some weeks or a couple of days, others are living abroad, but there is an inner connection.

Some have gone a long way in their spiritual search.

But not all the people who gather around a Sufi teacher are serious seekers.

Some of them are only looking for a personal authority or merely contact or any kind of esoteric knowledge.

Nevertheless, everyone is welcome to begin with, receives an introduction into the practice of meditation and then has to continue on his own.

A real Sufi student is above all moved by longing and yearning for Truth, Understanding, The One, The Absolute, Love, Nothingness — concepts and names are of no importance.

"The Tao that can be described is not the true Tao." (*Tao te king*)

A Sufi student learns at first how little he really understands and knows, he or she recognizes how his thinking and behavior patterns obstruct development.

Apart from the spiritual path, every Sufi aspirant has to take his place in human society, in his family and his job. Everyone has to be a useful member of the society.

Sufis are not in this life for personal reasons.

And they do not strive only for spiritual understanding, they have to refer to every aspect of life: their relationships and partners, family life, job, duties and responsibilities.

In all areas the first concern for a Sufi aspirant is to bring order into daily life. Sufism is no escape from the difficulties of life. Being a Sufi you have to accept all aspects of life and have to be seriously involved with love, thus discovering the divine hints and the divine presence everywhere.

The Sufi Group

In former times there were Dervish orders and Sufi tariquats. They have become the modern Sufi groups. The Sufi community is a place to offer mutual help and assistance and growth, a spiritual brotherhood and sisterhood. Sufi groups are determined by the commitment to the same goal and meditation practice.

Their cohesion is not based on a we-feeling or determined by sympathy; the cohesion of the group comes from the energy field and power originated by the master and by the common meditation practice.

On one hand, you can find all the social psychological phenomena and group dynamics seen in any other group; on the other hand Sufi groups are very special.

They are essentially open and welcoming communities. The group cares for the problems of members, newcomers or guests. There are no ritual conditions for membership, inclusion is based on the attraction to the Sufi path, which finds it physical expression in the person of the master.

Study work in a Sufi group is unpredictable: there is group meditation (in our group it is a silent meditation which activates the heart-chakra), working with dreams, discussing problems, cracking Sufi jokes (a Sufi without humour is totally impossible), laughing, having tea together, telling stories, lectures of the teacher, empathy, communion in silence.

The atmosphere in a Sufi group is warmhearted, peaceful and relaxed. Only in a relaxed presence, here and now attachment and stress can go and deeper experiences of stillness and meditation are possible.

The Sufi community doesn't create boundaries towards others. It is a model for a real community of human beings.

Sufi groups are not institutionalized. They are meaningful instruments only for a present situation.

Of course sometimes there are frictions between people, but Sufis are trained to be patient with human shortcomings, to recognize in the mirror of the thou one's own shadow problems. Sufis have to learn to take back projections, to be patient with oneself and others and to give up personal importance, that is, the ego.

Apart from group meditation there are no fixed rules in our Sufi group in London.

We never know what will happen, who will be present or what will be discussed or done.

This is also a way to learn how to remain open to the present moment and how to deny needs for security and rigid habits.

Thus Sufi training is completely unpredictable. But first of all, it is learning how to learn, being in contact with others, becoming more and more silent and open in meditation. Sufi groups are laboratories for human transformation. It is here where the Sufis are cooked with the energies of love. Sufism is the path of the loving heart.

The Sufi Path

There are numerous descriptions of the levels and phases of development in Sufi literature.

I would like to name some steps in terms of contemporary psychology:
— Orientation and attraction by Sufism
— Learning how to learn
— Deconditioning, deprogramming (analytical and therapeutic work)
— Balancing the inner and outer world (In-tuition, inner experiences through meditation, expanding consciousness)
— Individuation, becoming who you are
— The power of love or being a lover
— Mystical experience of Oneness and Nothingness.

For Sufi students Jungian Psychology is very helpful, because it is a system open to transcendence and what Jung called the "Numinous".

Thus we can say a modern Western Sufi has to go, first of all, the psychological way of individuation.

But then he has to transcend the frontier at which Jung stopped and which is the limitation of psychological understanding. Sufis are psychologists and experts of the human psyche, but above all they are mystics. Their goal is not individuation but the realization of God.

Sufis as Lovers

All mystics describe their experience of God in the language and with images of intimate embrace, as a union in love.

Rumi, the great Persian Sufi says: "Wherever you are and however you feel, always tend to be a lover."

Love is the universal power of transformation. On the Sufi path, love is generated from heart to heart by the spiritual teacher. It is the opening of the heart chakra that is given highest attention. Preparing yourself and emptying yourself is done in meditation. Love is experienced as an intense suffering of separation from the Beloved. It is longing and a burning desire beyond all reason. On the path, the Sufi student learns to perceive the different forms of love, to make more and more empty space for love.

"Love is quenching the thirst on the physical plane. This is not love. The human being is love, and Love loves the human being. To realize Love is to realize God. If we sit before an open fire, it warms us. There is no effort on our part. Those who have realized God are like this fire. Keep in their company. God realized Himself in the heart of Hearts of the human being. Example of the ocean and the waves. They disappear and are here. When we realize, Love disappears. We cannot give shape or name to Love. the deeper we go, the more it disappears. It radiates from every part of the body. And the last transfer which takes place from the Master to the disciple is from the heart to the heart. Where the trouble comes from, help is also there; people forget it, that's why they are in trouble."

"Everything is done with spiritual power on our Line."(I. Tweedie, 1986, p. 517)

Genuine understanding on the Sufi path is gained only through love. Saint Augustine declares the same: "You can recognize something only to the extent you love it." (Res tantum cognoscitur quantum diligitur.)

And for all searching seekers, Kabir's word might offer some comfort: "I am wandering yet in the alleys of knowledge without purpose, but I have received His news in these alleys of knowledge. I have a letter from my Beloved: in this letter is an unutterable message, and now my fear of death is gone away."

References

C.G. Jung. **Gesammelte Werke**. Walter Verlag, Olten, 1971

Songs of Kabir, translated by Rabindranath Tagore. Samuel Weiser Inc., New York, 1981

Shah, I. **Die Sufis**. Dusseldorf, Diederichs, 1981

Shah, I. **The Way of The Sufi**. Penguin Books Ltd., Harmondsworth, England, 1974

Shah, I. **Learning How to Learn**. Octagon Press, London, 1978

Schimmel, A. Mystische Dimensionen des Islam. Qualandar Verlag, Aalen, 1979

Tart, Ch. **Transpersonal Psychologies**. Harper & Row Publishers, Inc., New York, 1975

Tweedie, I. **Daughter of Fire**. Blue Dolphin Publishing Inc., Nevada City, 1986

This article is based upon my own experiences in the Sufi group of Irina Tweedie. She got her initiation and training from her Guru in India according to the Sufi way of the Naqshbandi line.

Author Birgitte Dorst, Dr. phil., clinical psychologist and psychotherapist, Professor of social psychology at the College of Applied Science and Arts in Cologne, West Germany, director of the Women studies program, has been in training as a Jungian analyst at the C. G. Jung Institute in Zurich since 1984.

In Search Of A Name

By Tasnim Fernandez

Hermila. (Pronounced Er-me-la). A rare name, and for a young Mexican girl in her new American home, a name that felt like a curse of alienation. In the small school that I attended in El Paso, Texas, almost none of the kids could pronounce my name and the teacher, too, managed to butcher it every time she spoke it. Still, I credit my name, Hermila, with bringing me to Sufism, my spiritual home.

In the Sufi Order of the West, founded by Pir-o-Murshid Inayat Khan, we utilize the practice of invocation of the Divine Qualities of God. We are taught that sound (vibration) is creative. Thus how we address each other and what we call our children, such as 'sweetie', 'angel', 'honey', or 'clumsy', 'stupid', 'good-for-nothing', etcetera, make an impression on the person and she or he begins to manifest that quality or 'name' which they've been called.

The foreignness of my name bothered me. I longed to have a "normal" name like Cathy or Susie or Judy. At home I was called Mila and, by some older relatives, in the diminutive: Milita. Even this was still too foreign so when my family moved to Los Angeles I changed my name. I won't tell you what name I chose since I don't want to send that vibration out anymore. I *will* tell you that during a time when I was singing with a small jazz combo that I used the name Lynn Parrish. Now that's really American-sounding! Anyone with some insight can see that I was not only eschewing my name but also trying to reject my Mexican heritage. It had given me so much pain in my earliest encounters with American life that I really just wanted to be an Anglo and to blend in. It had been the "white" kids in El Paso who teased and made fun of all the little brown kids with the strange-sounding names. The cruelty of bigotry and prejudice is unmitigated among children.

As I matured I slowly began to reclaim my inheritance until, by my early twenties, I again became Hermila. At about the same time I became interested in metaphysical ideas which, combined with the intrigue that the name 'Hermila' still held for me, lead to my investigation of Alchemy and Hermetics. I used to wonder whether 'Hermila' was etymologically connected with 'Hermes'. And although

I was named after my paternal grandmother, even my father didn't know anything about the name. I read on and since I was new to metaphysics there were many things that I didn't understand but that didn't deter me from going deeper into such books attributed to Hermes Trismegistus as *The Divine Pymander* and *The Emerald Tablets of Hermes Trismegistus*. Then one day I received an announcement of a lecture being offered on "Alchemy and the Kabbalah" by a man named Pir Vilayat Khan. Of course, I went.

As I've said, I was a neophyte, so as I sat there listening to the lecture, complete with diagrams of the Kabbalistic sephiroth, I felt as though these ancient mysteries were wafting over and past my head like the most delicate soap bubbles. I knew they were treasures but I couldn't quite grasp them. What was really overwhelming, however, was the bearing and presence of the man presenting the lecture. He was soft-spoken yet firm and confident in his delivery and there was such gracefulness about his manner and an air of...well, of nobility. I couldn't take my eyes off of him and I contrived some insignificant "question" to ask him after the talk so that I could come into closer contact with him. He responded kindly and that was that. I went home and within some short time I had forgotten about him.

About a year later I found myself in a deep state of despair. My relationship had taken a turn for the worse. As I stood at the kitchen sink, my eyes red and swollen from crying all night, looking out of the window into the dawning morning I felt as though my life was falling apart. I was several months pregnant and what had been a pure joy was now overshadowed by fear. I didn't know how our relationship, if there was going to be one, would ever survive. My lover and mate had been out all night and I was quite sure where he'd been all night, with whom. As I felt more and more hopelessness, depression and abandonment it was as though I was in the midst of a black cave with no exit. Suddenly, through all the darkness and misery that surrounded me, there came a brilliant sense of light and in the middle of the light stood Pir Vilayat Khan, the man whom I had heard and seen and had forgotten. He was the light. He represented a 'way out'. Then I knew that I had to find him. This is no easy task when one sets out to find a Sufi...they can't be found. After much diligence I contacted a lovely, elderly French lady who was the local contact for Pir (elder) Vilayat. She loaned me my first Sufi book to read and in a very casual, almost off-handed manner she said that if I had any questions that I should feel free to call on her again.

As I read the book, one of the volumes of the Sufi Message by Pir-o-Murshid Inayat Khan (Pir Vilayat's father), I found myself responding with near total agreement. It felt as though I was reading my own sentiments and thoughts. I was home. There was no need to convert to anything; I had always had this philosophy! So I returned to see my friend and mentor, Ms. Bibijan, and we spent long hours in her little flower garden talking about 'life'. Then she told me that Pir Vilayat would soon be giving a weekend retreat and that I could attend if I wanted to. By now my daughter had been born and although her father and I were still together the relationship was still fraught with troubles. I made my decision to attend the retreat. Once again I was in that awesome presence. There was so much that I didn't understand. The terminology was almost the least of it! The truly foreign aspect of the experience was the deep quietude that I felt. I was in another realm. One that I hadn't experienced so palpably before.

Then I asked for initiation. I didn't really know what I was asking for or what it meant. I just knew, with full certainty, that Pir Vilayat was my teacher. I felt that the beauty, insight, peace and majesty which he exhibited was somehow now accessible to *me* and that I too could possibly aspire to attain these qualities *as a human being* here on earth. For, after all, sitting before me was a mortal man who had made great strides in his spiritual evolution and I believed that I could learn from him. Bibijan walked with me into the room where the initiations were being given. She whispered a word or two to Pir then she withdrew to the back of the room. She was my sponsor and my witness. I will never forget her. Standing before Pir Vilayat, he held my hands and asked me several questions. I felt truly unworthy! Yet he gave me his hands, physically and spiritually. To be received as his mureed (student) felt like the greatest kindness and magnanimity that anyone could have extended to me. As he blessed me my eyes filled with tears. I tried to look at him but I couldn't, his light was blinding (or was it the salt of my tears?) and I felt that he saw right through me. He spoke to me a bit more and recommended a practice which I immediately forgot. I am so glad that Bibijan was there to remind me later of what he had said. I must say that I, like so many other people, assumed that now that I was initiated that my life would be wonderful and that all of my problems would disappear. Of course they didn't, and they don't. We all are here to grow from life's experiences and I had unknowingly chosen a path that emphasizes life *in* the world. This school does not encourage the monastic or hermetic life. We do use retreats as a means of withdrawing from the concerns of daily life so that we may dive deeply into the falseness of our small, restricted identity. But it is done in order to reclaim our divine inheritance, not as an escape from life. Now my readings in alchemy and hermetics came to a fuller light as I experienced the stages of the alchemical retreat process developed by Pir Vilayat. Now what I had held in my mind as theory became a fully experienced reality. In the first stages of the retreat process we utilize the alchemical model which describes the dissolution (*solve*) of the dross; the *notion* of who we are stands in the way of who we might be if we would be what we could be. After the stages of dissolution come the stages of coagulation. One could also put this process in the Christian terminology of crucifixion and resurrection. Something has to die for the new birth to occur. And the image of the sacred marriage, the material-ization of spirit and the spiritualization of matter happens *in us* ! We are the laboratory for this alchemy. From the dross of our limited 'self' we distill the essence and give birth to or bring forth the gold of our real 'Self'. (I find it interesting that the English word "Real" translates as "royal" in Spanish.)

My studies in Sufism continued and I had applied much of the teachings to my life. I had gotten to a point where I received a lot of recognition and praise for my classes and the teaching work that I was doing. But inside I saw myself like a bush that grows naturally and what I had done with this natural, untrained bush was to trim it, nurture it, dig around the trunk and, symbolically speaking, I had tended it so well that there was outer praise and recognition for the lovely bush. Still, I had a gnawing feeling that the roots, the level beneath the visible, were tangled and moulding. There was much more "subterranean" work to be done.

I had gone to Phoenix to present a weekend workshop when, on the first night there, I had a deeply moving dream. The feeling of the dream was as if present with me for several days. And I felt very sure of the initiatic nature of the dream. Once more I was to embark on an unknown journey toward my true self.

The Dream

I was walking behind a robed and hooded figure that seemed to float rather than to walk across beautiful mosaic floors. The figure, which I call the Spirit of Guidance, lead me through expansive, open rooms with crystal chandeliers, marble columns, long, winding staircases, gilded ornaments and richly woven tapestries. We moved in silence through this opulence. Suddenly we stopped. We were in front of a great door. Then, for the first time, the spirit "spoke" to me. I heard every word clearly, or perhaps more accurately, I perceived every word with my whole being. The Spirit of Guidance turned to me and said, "This is where I take leave of you. If you choose, you may open this door. The choice is solely yours and there is no right and no wrong choice. Either choice is of equal weight. If you choose to open the door and to enter, I will meet you on the other side." Then the Spirit of Guidance was gone and I was alone facing THE DOOR, left with MY CHOICE. I was trembling as I took hold of the doorknob. I knew that I *must* open the door. There *was* no other choice. As I pulled the door open I stepped into the darkest, blackest unknown that I had ever faced. I took a breath in and exhaled as I took my first step into the darkness. I was engulfed by the black and couldn't see anything; nothing at all was visible, not even my own body. After a few steps I began to feel soothed. There was a sense of a comforting presence in the darkness and I felt as though voices were speaking to me, saying, "Do not fear. All who have gone before you through the darkness guide and comfort you now. We are with you and with every traveler in this way." The feeling was as if there were arms and hands gently, sweetly touching me, reassuring me, giving me strength with their touch. I knew that I would make it. When I awoke I was ecstatic. The ecstasy stayed with me for several days. And when I returned to Los Angeles I told a friend about the dream and she excitedly said that she knew a woman to whom I should tell this dream. It turned out that the woman worked as an art therapist and she was very much inclined toward Jungian psychology. That was the beginning of my journey into the world of C.G. Jung. I read many of his works, difficult though they were. I attended lectures, workshops, and I embarked on this new journey into the realm of depth psychology.

Over the last seven years I have discovered many correlations between my Sufi studies and my inner plunging into the depths of my psyche. I am grateful that I have both paths upon which to journey just as I am grateful that I have two eyes, two ears, two hands, two feet. I am working toward balance (the keynote of the Sufi message is Balance). And I am working toward integration of the opposite aspects of my being.

I found it interesting to read in Jung's writings that often his analysands would rediscover, or perhaps come to for the first time, a sense of the holy or of the spiritual in life, some of them returning to a religion that they may have discarded earlier. I happened to have come to psychoanalysis already deeply engaged in the spiritual life, therefore, I always had available a support for the disquieting and

sometimes painful encounters with my buried past. I have found that
Jung and Sufism are very compatible for me. Pir Vilayat often says that
our Order does not encourage the use of spirituality as a "by-pass" to
the exigencies of life and I was glad not to have had to conform to an
idea that all things can and *ought* to be handled through spiritual
practices. Sometimes a *doctor* is called for, not a *priest.* And sometimes
the warmth and understanding of a loving (spiritual) heart is the best
"medicine". The wisdom is in knowing whom to call for which
condition.

Biographical

I was educated in the United States, mostly in California, up to the
second year of college. My main areas of study and interest were in
Music, Art, Theater and English. I'm amazed by the confluence of events
that show a wisdom acting within and beyond my own "intention". I
had thought at different times in my life that I wanted to be a teacher,
a nun, a social worker, a singer...and, lo and behold, I turned out to be a
teacher, a spiritual guide and counselor and to use music as one of my
primary modes of teaching, The Dances of Universal Peace. I sing and
dance with others for the elevation of humanity and the glory of God. I
have traveled in France, Germany, Switzerland, Turkey, and most
recently have been privileged to share the Dances of Universal Peace
in the Soviet Union. Every experience in life can become a skill or a tool
for the betterment of our selves and, consequently, for the betterment of
all life. I am deeply grateful for and indebted to all the people in my
life, bar none! Everyone has been my teacher. I pray that I may always
be a good student.

Although I am a member of several Sufi Orders and other esoteric
schools I would rather that they remain anonymous for it is no
particular credit to me that I have been so blessed and do not wish to
use these blessings as one would use and display one's merit badges.

I am now known as Tasnim Hermila Fernandez. I have grown into my
name of birth and I now also possess the most beautiful and inspiring
spiritual name, Tasnim: the fountain of Supreme Exaltation which is to
be found in the Garden of Paradise. I am deeply proud of my Mexican
heritage and am most grateful to my parents for having made possible
for me such a wonderful life. I am grateful to Pir Vilayat Inayat Khan
whose very light guided me from the deepest darkness to the One
Light.

C.G. Jung & Sufism

By Pir Vilayat Inayat Khan

"Whatever we know today is the result of thousands of years of experience. The discovery of the very least thing is the discovery of the whole of humanity. The whole of humanity has shared in everything that we think new today." Hazrat Inayat Khan[1]

"There is a still deeper sphere to which our memory is linked, and that is the only sphere of the universal memory, in other words the divine mind... Only for this the doors of memory should be laid open... The storehouse of which I spoke of is the subconscious mind. In that storehouse there are things and they live." Hazrat Inayat Khan[2]

"Ultimately they are all founded on primordial *archetypal forms* whose concreteness dates from a time when consciousness did not think but only perceived...we also have a pre-existent thinking, of which we are not aware." Jung[3]

For a Sufi scholar, browsing through the monumental plethora of C. G. Jung's literary legacy, even the most perfunctory perusal strikes a resonant note as meaningful parallels flash through one's mind.

Foremost, both Jung and the Sufis seek access to no-man's lands beyond the middle range compass of the psyche where a sense of meaningfulness is attained that defies our common-place thinking yet may prove decisive in one's self image. Both Jung and the Sufis nurture a holistic view of the psyche, thus eluding the simplistic reductionist

---

[1] **The Message of Hazrat Inayat Khan**, published by the International Headquarters of the Sufi Movement, volume VII p. 224. Cf. Pir Vilayat Inayat Khan, **The Message in our Time**, Harper & Row, 1979, p. 108.

[2] Hazrat Inayat Khan op. cit. Volume IV p. 137.

[3] C.G. Jung, **The Archetypes of the Collective Unconscious**, Bollingen Series, Princeton, U.S.A., 1980, p. 33.

view which fails to include the wider dimensions of one's being in one's self-image, and by the same token one's world view.

> "Although she, the 'anima', may be the chaotic lure to life, something strangely meaningful clings to her, a secret knowledge or inner wisdom which contrasts most curiously with her irrational elfin nature." Jung [4]

> "Interpretations are only for those who don't understand; it is only the things that we don't understand that have any meaning." Jung[5]

Although they do not use the word individuation, for the Sufis, the human being is the fulfillment of the divine purpose, or more precisely: the objective of the universe is that the bounty of the potentials of the totality (present and virtual) be increasingly actuated in the individual as humanity mutates in the course of the evolutionary process, at least in the purview of Planet Earth.

> "The development of one's personality is the real purpose of life." Hazrat Inayat Khan[6]

Therefore their quest for the higher dimensions of their being is not motivated by an intent on attaining liberation from the human existential condition, but rather to incorporate the bounty of these higher counterparts of their being into their personality to make them into an existential reality.

> "If there had not been a desire and hope for the fruit, how would the gardener have planted the root of the tree? ...the branch came into existence for the sake of the fruit" Jelal ud Din Rumi[7]

> "But for pure love, how should I have given existence to the celestial spheres?" Jelal ud Din Rumi [8]

---

[4] Op. cit. p. 30.
[5] Op. cit. p. 31.
[6] Op. cit. IV p. 106.
[7] William C. Chittick, **The Sufi Path of Love,** State of University of New York Press, Albany, N.Y., p. 67.
[8] Masnavi 2736-40, Vide William C. Chittick, op. cit. p. 198.

"And God said: 'Thou' is the purpose of the whole of the phenomenal existence." Niffari[9]

"The human personality is the fruit on the tree of life...or...you may think of yourself as a plant in which only little of the bounty latent in the seed is manifest, yet in this plant, the seed that caused the whole existence — God — is to be found." Hazrat Inayat Khan[10]

"The purpose of the whole of creation is fulfilled in the attainment of that perfection which is for a human being to attain." Hazrat Inayat Khan[11]

For both Carl Jung and the Sufis, these cosmic potentials which defy our minds manifest to the psyche in the form of symbols which furnish clues to the unfathomable and inexhaustible archetypes of the software of the human psyche. But for the Sufis, sometimes they reveal themselves in the features of the countenance in his/her subtle body.

For Shihabuddin Suhrawardhi there is a way of looking upon the earth: rather than perceiving it through the senses, one contemplates a precognitive image inherent in one's soul. The scene on the earth triggers off this image which lays latent in one. One's mind belongs to the sphere of Hyrkalya, the sphere where creative imagination moulds the archetypes of those forms which are eventually projected as objects or bodies of planets or galaxies.

"Since these images in one's imagination carry the hallmark of the angels who projected them, and since one's soul is an angel and reflects the archetypal images of the archangels of light and splendor, these forms in the mind will concur with the images that one carries in one's soul." H. Corbin[12]

"Sensory matter is but the vehicle, or rather the epiphanic place for the forms produced by the activity of the soul...this does not mean knowing things as abstract idea, as philosophical concept, but as the perfectly individuated features of their Image meditated, or rather pre-meditated by

---

[9] **The Mawaqif and Mukhatabat of Muhammad ibn'l-Jabbar al'Niffari,** edited A.J. Arberry, Luzac & Co., London, W.C., p. 30.

[10] Extract from public lecture.

[11] **The Sufi Message of Hazrat Inayat Khan,** volume XI, p. 356.

[12] Vide H. Corbin: **Spiritual Body and Celestial Earth,** Bollingen, Princeton University Press, p. 4.

the soul, namely their archetypal Image...this means in effect, that if things corresponding to all these are visible and seen in this world here, on this terrestrial earth, it is because ultimately what we call physics, physical is but the reflection of the world of the soul...there is no pure physics, but always the physics of some definite psychic activity. So to become aware of it is to see the world of the soul, to see all things as they are in the Earth of Hurqalya the world of archetypal images." H. Corbin[13]

Reading the following, words of Prof. H. Corbin, one would hasten to infer that these were indeed the words of Jung.

"Preceding all empirical data, the archetype Images are the organs of meditation of the active Imagination: they effect the transmutation of these data by giving them their meaning...and precisely by so doing make known the manner of being of a specific human presence and the fundamental orientation inherent in it." H. Corbin[14]

As we see, Corbin stresses the particularity of each human unconscious respectively rather than their universality.

"One notices in fact a certain tendency to accentuate in this expression the adjective 'collective', to the point of giving it the substantiality and virtues of an hypothesis; in so doing it is simply forgotten that the purpose of psycho-analysis is as therapy for the soul, tends to foster what it called the process of individuation. For the same reason, it would be absurd to explain the kind of individual initiation proper to Sufism by relating it to some collective norm, whereas its whole purpose is to free the inner man from such authority." Corbin[15]

"The Power that is in thee, in each one of you, cannot refer to a collective guide, to a manifestation and a relationship collectively identical for each one of the souls of light. Nor a fortiori can it be the macrocosm or universal man (Insan kolli) which assumes the role of heavenly counterpart of each microcosm." Corbin[16]

---

13 Op. cit. p. 81.

14 **The Man of Light in Iranian Sufism,** Shambala, p. 5.

15 Op. cit. p. 95.

16 Op. cit. p. 16.

"Whether it is referred to as the divine Being or as the archetype angel, no sooner does its apparition reveal the transcendent dimension of spiritual individuality as such that it must take on individualized features and establish an individuated relationship." Corbin[17]

It follows that, while C. G. Jung ascribes these archetypes to a collective dimension of the individual, rather on the model of the holographic paradigm, the Sufis highlight the super celestial dimension of the person as unique for each person.

"By no means is it an allegorical construct, but a primordial Image thanks to which the seeker perceives a world of realities which is neither the world of senses nor the world of abstract concepts." Corbin[18]

Accessing these surreptitiously when the censorship of the unconscious is off-guard during sleep, one has a means of integrating them into the conscious. This he calls individuation. The Sufis explore the areas of the psyche in the act of contemplation. This occurs by keeping oneself suspended at the threshold between sleep and day consciousness, leaving as it were, the door ajar between those two very different perspectives. Like Jung, their objective is to integrate the values thus encompassed into the personality creatively. Recognizing several levels within this paradoxical 'unconscious', they try to discern their counterpart corresponding to each of the levels mapped by the contemplatives. These counterparts or alter-egos appear to them as subtle bodies. Then in a further step, they try to restructure these bodies on the model of their higher self.

As in the case of Jung, for the Sufis, access to these 'higher levels' of one's being, at least in the initial stages, needs to be mediated through images, by-passing the conceptual mind.

"The symbolic process is an experience in images and of images; and its goal is broadly speaking illumination or higher consciousness by means of which the initial situation is overcome on a higher level." Jung[19]

However, while Jung's main focus as a therapist is on therapy, the Sufi contemplatives foster creativity by cultivating that 'organ' of

---

[17] Op. cit. p. 20.
[18] Op. cit. p. 32.
[19] **The Archetypes.** p. 38-39.

creativity which they coin 'creative imagination'. In this respect it appears that the processes they initiate are complementary, so that a cross-pollination of the two terms of the Janus polarity of the psyche may well open new perspectives.

But it is at this point that we encounter the differences in the techniques applied respectively. Whereas Jung interprets the dreams of his patients, pointing out the relevance of the symbols encountered in the dream experience, Ibn 'Arabi, Shihabuddin Suhrawardhi, amongst many other Sufis, practice a form of lucid dreaming that one might call reverie. So that instead of the unconscious communicating to the conscious clues to its message by dint of symbols, the consciousness of the Sufi contemplative wanders in the paradoxical and sometimes ambivalent areas of the unconscious which he/she envisions as being the celestial, sometimes super-celestial spheres.

Corbin's criticism consists in that he doubts that Jung considers the archetypal level as a concrete reality or sphere beyond the physical universe that may actually be reached.

"The inability to conceive of a concrete supra-sensory reality results from giving too much importance to sensory reality; this view, generally speaking, leaves no alternative but to take the supra-sensory universe as consisting of abstract concepts. On the contrary, the universe which in Suhrawardhi's neo-Zoroastrian Platonism is called the mundus imaginalis ('alam al-mithal) or the 'heavenly Earth of Huralya' is a concrete spiritual universe." Corbin[20]

"Najm Kobra describes real events which take place in the inner world on the plane of visionary apperception, in an order of perception corresponding specifically to the organ of perception which is the imaginative faculty." Corbin[21]

Upon reflection, what does one mean by concrete reality? Here we come up against the perennial catch-22 or Schroedinger's cat. Must reality be objective (the object of sensorial experience of the mental or emotional contents of the psyche) to be real? The Sufis make a clear distinction between purely subjective impression and the actual experience availed of by the act of the imaginative faculty. They ascribe this experience to a concrete reality that has its seat on higher planes and exists regardless of his/her perception thereof. Moreover

---

[20] **The Man of Light**, p. 5.
[21] Op. cit. p. 64.

they concentrate more particularly upon our personal heavenly counterpart rather than the impersonal dimension of our psyche coined by Jung the collective unconscious.

However, as one rises from one plane to the next (from 'alam al mithal', through 'alam al malakut' and 'alam al Jabur'), one encounters counterparts that become less personal and more universal. While at the plane 'alam al mithal', one discovers one's dream personality as being very different from one's familiar terrestrial one, and at the level of 'al malakut', one's counterpart appears in the form of an angel; at the plane 'aljabarut', it is pure splendor beyond form, and at the level of 'al lahut lahut' as one discovers the sphere of the archetypal seminal attributes, one discovers the universal and perfect dimensions of one's being. According to Hazrat Inayat Khan this is the level at which our divine inheritance originates; here is the model to be found of which our personality is simply an exemplar.

Therefore, insofar as individuation means the integration of the cosmic dimension of our being into our personality, it starts according to the Sufis at a level above the one they would assign to our psyche.

Perhaps we may distinguish the difference or rather the complementarity of the two points of view here being confronted as that between the cosmic and the transcendental dimensions — may I say vectors? — of our being, as a matter of fact of all reality. The cosmic dimension may be represented by the holistic paradigm: inasmuch as it is possible to fragment a crystal, each fraction functions after the same manner as the whole crystal albeit less efficiently. Whereas the transcendental dimension could be illustrated by the relationship between a model and its exemplars, or better still the software and the hardware of the universe. I propose the following mathematical formulations: Cosmic 1=infinity divided by infinity; transcendental 1=1 to the power infinity.

But one can only surmise the nature of the archetype through the exemplar, unless, as Ibn'Arabi says, one switches over one's vantage point so that one sees God through God's eyes. Indeed, the knowledge gleaned by grasping in oneself the divine archetype is only the first degree of the Sufi.

"You know yourself with another knowledge different from
that which you had when you knew your Lord by the

knowledge that you had of yourself; for now it is through Him that you know yourself." Ibn 'Arabi[22]

One might add this knowledge is the one that God has of Himself through you.

However, comparisons often miss out recognizing similarities; in fact Jung appears to grasp in the very universality of the collective unconscious some kind of argument in favour of some realness. Indeed if several people have similar or identical experiences, one tends to infer that we have to do with something which by-passes whimsical phantasies, even if we are talking about a subjective reality — therefore present in our psyche. Whereas for the Sufis, their existence cannot be reduced to the psyche, albeit they can only be gleaned through the act of the imaginative faculty.

For example Avicenna and Suhrawardhi distinguish clearly in their visionary experiences between the landscapes of the soul they explore and their own effigy, besides the beings whom they encounter. Yet in the last analysis these beings and landscapes aver themselves as aspects of their own selves.

"The mystical experience is the intimate feeling that an event is taking place within you. This transmutation includes a transmutation of the faculties of sensory perception." Najm Kobra[23]

Yet does Jung really ascribe the archetypes to mere abstractions rather than a prime reality having its existence sui generis outside our perception of these? The following quote seems to invalidate that view:

"The eternal ideas are primordial images stored up in a super celestial place as eternal transcendental forms. The eye of the seers perceives them as images in dreams and revelatory visions. Ultimately they are all founded on primordial archetypal forms whose concreteness dated from a time when consciousness did not think but only perceived...thought was essentially revelation, not invented but forced upon us or bringing conviction through its immediacy and actuality...we

---

[22] Vide Henri Corbin: **Creative Imagination in the Sufism of Ibn' Arabi,** Princeton University, p. 133.

[23] Vide Corbin, **The Man of Light,** p. 80.

also have a pre-existent thinking of which we are not aware so long as we are supported by traditional symbols." Jung[24]

"Only when all props and crutches are broken and no cover from the rear offers even the slightest hope of security, does it become possible to experience an archetype that up to then had lain hidden behind the meaningful nonsense played out by the anima...in all chaos there is cosmos; in all disorder a secret order; in all caprice, a fixed law."[25]

In this connection, Sufism corroborates and even substantiates Jung's view by referring personal impressions back to their archetypal dimension:

"To see or perceive things in Hurkalya... The bringing into play of this faculty is designated by the technical term 'tawil', which etymologically means 'to bring back' the data to their origin, to their archetype, to their donor. For this, the same data must be recaptured at each of the degrees of being or levels through which they had to 'descend' in order to reach the mode of being corresponding to the plane on which they are evident to our ordinary consciousness... Hence the ta'wil is preeminently the hermeneutics of symbols, the ex-egus, the bringing out of hidden spiritual meaning...there would be no possibility of a ta'wil without the world of hurqalya, which we are at present studying; that is without the world of archetypal images where that imaginative perception functions and is able, by transmuting the material data of external history into symbols, to penetrate to the inner meaning." Corbin[26]

"The advantage of dreams over the positive data of waking life is that they permit or rather require, an interpretation that transcends all data, for data signify something other than what is disclosed... The initial imaginative operation is to typify the immaterial and spiritual realities in external or sensuous forms, which then become 'ciphers' for what they manifest." Corbin[27]

---

[24] **The Archetypes,** op. cit. p. 33.

[25] Op. cit. p. 32.

[26] **Spiritual Body and Celestial Earth** p. 53.

[27] **Creative Imagination,** p. 208-209.

Concerns about differences fade away positively when the following quotes are brought in parallel:

"To speak of the polar dimension as the transcendent dimension of the earthly individuality is to point out that it includes a counterpart, a 'heavenly partner', and that its total structure is a bi-unity, a unus-ambos. The unus-ambos can be taken as an alternation of the first and second person, as forming a dialogical unity thanks to the identity of their essence and yet without confusion of the persons. This is why the polar dimension is heralded in the guise of a Figure whose recurrent manifestations correspond on each occasion to an absolutely personal experience of the spiritual seeker and to the realization of this bi-unity." Corbin[28]

"But to have a soul is the whole venture of life. It is something that lives of itself that makes us live; it is a life behind consciousness that cannot be completely integrated with it but from which on the contrary consciousness arises." Jung[29]

Consequently the experiences of the dreamer assumes the form of landscapes in which they have the impression of advancing and in which they recognize themselves. These are obviously projections of their own being in the form of a scenario, thus providing them with a kind of psycho-feed-back system. Landscapes are of course encountered in the dreams reported by Jung.

"But the process itself involves another class of archetypes which one could call the archetypes of transformation. They are not personalities, but are typical situations, places, ways and means, that symbolizes the kind of transformation in question." Jung[30]

However at some point the landscapes seem to be populated with beings, obviously their alter ego appearing as another person.

"In the course of this process, the archetypes appear as active personalities in dreams and phantasies." Jung[31]

---

[28] **The Man of Light,** p. 7-8.
[29] **The Archetypes,** p. 27.
[30] Op. cit. p. 38.
[31] Op. cit. p. 38.

In many cases, this figure is inspiring, superlative, a perfect model or prototype of their own being whom they fail to identify with, who has a patronizing attitude and assumes the function of a guide and ultimately reveals him/herself as their own higher being. The act of recognition is then mirrored.

"I go towards my likeness, and my likeness goes towards me. He embraces me and holds me close as if I had come out of prison."[32]

"Each of the two assumes the position of the I and the self-image: my image looks at me with my gaze and I look at it with its own gaze." Majriti[33]

"For he contemplates you with the same look with which you contemplate him." Nasir ud Din Tusi[34]

"I see Him through His eyes and He sees me through my eyes. The being who knows is the very same being in whom He knows Himself." Ibn 'Arabi[35]

"I am the mirror of thy face; through thine own eyes, I look upon my countenance." Semnani[36]

"Not being is the mirror, the world the reflection, and you are as the reflected eye of the Unseen Person. In that eye, His eye sees His own eye." Mahmood Shabistari[37]

To discover an absolutely identical finding in Jung is a heartening confirmation of the universality of human experience in its deepest ground.

"When I experience the other in myself and the other in myself experiences me...there I am the object of every subject in complete reversal of my ordinary consciousness where I am

---

[32] Cf. E.S. Drowser, **The Mandaens of Iraq and Iran,** Oxford 1937, pp. 54-55.

[33] Vide Corbin **The Man of Light,** p. 17.

[34] Vide Corbin op. cit. p. 91.

[35] Vide H. Corbin, **Creative Imagination.** Bollingen, Princeton, N.J., 1969, p. 128.

[36] Vide Corbin, op. cit. p. 106.

[37] E. H. Whinffield: **Mahmood Shabistari's Gulshan i Raz,** tr. E.H. Whinfield, Trubner & Co., London (1880) p. 15.

always the subject that has an object. The unconscious no sooner touches me that touches us that we are it." Jung[38]

For the Sufis,

"The potentiality of the I is not itself without its other 'I'...the Figure that makes him see himself, because it is through his own eyes that the Figure looks at him." Corbin[39]

This Sufis emphasize the importance of rendering these qualities encountered at the higher levels of one's being corporeal:

"All these are illuminations which rise over the human soul when it is master of its body. Then they are reflected on the body habitation, the temple." Shihabuddin Yahya Suhrawardi[40]

One may ask what point is there in actualizing our celestial counterparts enjoying an eternal nature into a body that is transient? But for Sheikh Ahsa'i:

"The hidden invisible element [of the body], its innerness survives; this is the spiritual body, which is not formed from the sub-lunar elements, but from the four elements of the world of Hurqalya, which are seventy times nobler and more precious than the elements of the terrestrial world."[41] "...with which the supra-celestial archetypal body will be reunited"[42]

It may be inferred that the subtle body enriches the supra-celestial body with the wisdom and know-how fed back from its experience of the existential plane through the physical body.

In some cases, particularly significantly the figure appears in the likeness of what Jung calls the shadow. For the Sufis, as in the case of Jung, the shadow needs to be identified, recognized and accepted as an essential factor in one's being.

The figures appearing in the visionary experience of Avicenna are aspects of his own being and the master whom he encounters and who represents his higher self points out to him that their physiognomies which represent the various facets of the countenance of his subtle body

---

[38] **The Archetypes,** p. 22.
[39] **The Man of Light,** p. 91 op. cit.
[40] Vide Corbin, **Celestial Earth,** p. 126.
[41] Vide Corbin, **Celestial Earth,** p. 198.
[42] Vide Corbin, op. cit. p. 190.

reveal to him something about his shadow self which he is invited to overcome.

The master says to him:

> "The science of physiognomy figures amongst those sciences that yield their dividends immediately, because it reveals to you that which each person conceals in the secrecy of their nature."[43] "...Those companions who loiter around you are bad company. You incur the danger that they should seduce you and you will remain a captive of their hold upon you, unless the divine protection reaches you and preserves you from their bad influence. "[44]

Thus the state of reverie or lucid dreaming provides one with a feedback by way of an effigy-revealing aspect of oneself so far unbeknown, enabling one to work with restructuring the subtle bodies, particularly the body of resurrection.

> "In each part of a man which has been purified, its counterpart of the same nature is reflected, for nothing can be seen but its like. Therefore when the esoteric nature indicated by a man's inclination and faculties has become pure, he contemplates therein whatever is of the same nature in the macrocosm. The same applies to the soul, the heart, the spirit, the transconsciousness, up to the arcanum, the innermost place where the divine attributes which intoxicate are unveiled, and where it can be said: 'I am his hearing, I am his sight.'"
> (Qur'an) Ali-e Hamadani[45]

> "Therefore if you envision a heaven, an earth, a sun, or star or a moon, know that this is because the particle in you which comes from that mine has become pure." Najm Kubra[46]

When asked to reveal his real nature, the guiding archetypal figure appearing to Abd el Karim al Jili under the guise of Khidr (the Islamic counterpart of Elijah) says:

> "I am transcendent reality...I am the secret of man in his act of existing, and I am the invisible one who is the object of worship. I am the vial that contains the Essences, and I am the

---

[43] **Le recit de Hayy ibn Yaqzan** (trad. Corbin), Teheran 1953.
[44] Op. cit. p.11.
[45] Vide Corbin op. cit. p. 69 op. cit. p. 91.
[46] Vide Corbin op. cit. p. 71.

multitude of tenuous threads projected forth as mediators. I am
the Shaikh with the divine nature, and I am the guardian of
the world of human nature. I cause myself to be in every concept
and to be manifest in every dwelling...appear epiphanized in
every form, and I make a sign visible in every Sura. My
condition is to be esoteric, unusual. My situation is to be the
Stranger, the traveler..." Abd el Karim al Jili[47]

In these cryptic inferences we recognize the elusive communications of
the unconscious to which Jung has relentlessly lent his being to the
utmost, or are we talking of a supra-celestial consciousness that so
overlaps with an infra-consciousness that it is well nigh impossible to
unravel them?

"They are genuine symbols precisely because they are
ambiguous, full of half-glimpsed meanings, and in the last
resort inexhaustible...their manifold meanings, their almost
limitless wealth of reference makes any unilateral formulation
impossible...paradoxical." Jung[48]

Or do we espy the difference between the poles of the antimony
super-conscious and sub-conscious?

"The super-conscious arises on the horizon of consciousness;
while the human soul rises over the darkness of the
unconscious." Avicenna[49]

Thus the Sufis outline clues to applying our creative imagination to
the shaping of our subtle or celestial bodies which eventually
restructure our personality and even the countenance transpiring
through our bodily expression. The technique consists in mobilizing the
cosmic dimension of our personal emotions into shaping the form of our
veiled inner countenance which they call the body of resurrection.

In fact we unwittingly flaunt several superimposed faces or
countenances and are embodied in several intermeshed subtle bodies.
These are elaborately detailed in a study by an Iranian Sufi Pir of the
last century, Sheikh Ahsen Ahsai of Kirman.[50] Should one keep in

---

[47] **Insaan al Kamil (The Universal Man)** vide Corbin, **Spiritual Body.**
p. 156.

[48] **The Archetypes,** p. 38.

[49] Corbin, **Avicenna and the Visionary Recital,** Bollingen Series,
Pantheon Books, New York 1960 II, Chapter 12.

[50] Cf.: H. Corbin: **The Man of Light in Iranian Sufism.**

touch with the cosmic emotion passing through one's own emotion, the chances are that one's mind will keep in touch with the divine mind where the unconscious proves more efficient than the conscious or impersonal will more effective than the personal will, and the transcendental faculties of our mind more apt than our more commonplace thinking.

The critical issue is that in the existential state the realization of this lofty level of our being permeates our commonplace thinking in the form of that paradoxical thinking we call intuition and, if we allow it to do so, it will transmute our conceptual thinking, lifting it beyond its inadequacies.

Therefore the work of the spiritual adept is somewhat of the nature of that quintessential alchemical work at the level of the psyche called Ars Regia, the royal art. The 'opus', the work we undertake as adepts consists in earmarking our subtle bodies, unfurling them and inter-connecting them so that the bounty in store in the higher bodies may rub off onto the lower ones, eventually the personality. The Sufi dervishes attune their consciousness to the levels described as typifying the celestial spheres descending in sequence.

Alam al Hahut:

The method advocated consists in trying to recollect one's pristine condition, somehow stirring out of deep sleep in the night of time, enshrouded in a spell of silence while echoes of the turbulence of the existential universe reach one as from afar, somewhat quintessentiated.

At this level, the impersonal compass of this dimension of one's being is where the differentiations that make for our personal individuality have not yet been unfurled. This is somewhat like the original state of the embryo called in biology the blastoma, where the cells are not yet differentiated. Therefore all the potentialities of the universe are virtually present. The Muslims call these the secret treasures. "I was a secret treasure and desired to be known, and therefore the universe is the means of my self-discovery" (Hadith of Prophet Mohammed). This is why Hazrat Inayat Khan calls it the condition of the divine perfection — our divine inheritance.

Alam al Jabarut:

At this stage our essence does not have a physiognomy but exists as pure splendor, that level of reality that manifests as beauty but which itself does not possess a form. It can be sensed when contemplation is carried beyond form which cannot be achieved either by the mind, or by creative imagination but by allowing oneself to be aroused by the emotion that moves the universe and stirs one's soul in its depths. The Sufis refer to a condition where the soul 'perceives' a non physical reality.

Alam al Malakut:

However, according to the Sufis, our supra-celestial being adjoins itself with a subtle body which is able to register and carry the imprints, not only of the physical or even etheric or astral planes, but of the plane where the archetypal principles behind all existential formative processes are to be found. The Sufis look upon it as the place where the divine treasures hidden behind their display as the universe, are manifested and actuated as beings prior to conception and after death. "And there is not a thing but with us are the treasures of it; and we do not send it down but in known measure." Qur'an.

Let us call it the level at which the software of the universe is being 'homonized' (to borrow an expression of R.P. Teilhard de Chardin). You may become aware of this level of your being when you awaken from the limitations of the middle range operations of your mind and begin to grasp meaningfulness without the support of the perception of a physical event or relying on your interpretation of situations, for example your personal problems. It represents a lofty level of thinking and emoting, and while being relevant to understanding, once again it can only be reached by the break-through of ecstasy at the moment of "aha': discovering the divine intention behind what we interpret as events.

Alam al Mithal:

Now we land at the level of the activity of creative imagination emerging subliminally at a collective scale to be customized by our personal inventiveness: the world of myth gives vent to the world of metaphor.

Imagination, the act of the psyche already starts there, but it affirms its independence from the existential field wherever it projects images that are not a replica of the perceived.

This is creativity. It is the opposite of interpreting the data of experience which is data processing. To this category of imagination belongs our self-representation: our self-image. According to the Sufis, any representation, self or other than self, creates streamers in the subtle fabric of 'alam al mithal' which might conceivably be a sort of light that does not fit into the physicist's definition of physical light.

By dwelling upon the imaginary form, reiterating the act of imagination, it gradually gels and becomes an effigy having some measure of resilience. It might even become adamant.

Thus the semblance assumed by the body of resurrection, the effigy as we shape it, will serve as a feed-back spurring us to adjust our personality to actuate our vision of the way we would like our effigy to look like. This is where we have the full extent of our choice our free will. Actually what we mean by spirituality is the search and cult and creativity of the sublime, which means participating in the divine act whereby the physical world is shaped to manifest the sublimity of the emotion driving the universe. "As above so below" is the Hermetic adage.

The physiognomy of the effigy thus spirited, hopefully recurrently improved, fluctuates however according to our attunements and the degree of our realizations as we move across the scenarios of our experience; therefore it would be a mistake to represent it as static. To validate its dynamic nature and its interaction and even interfusion with the physical and psychological environment, indeed including the whole universe, it is incumbent (rather than to envision a statue-like effigy) to envision our effigy in movement, for example wandering in a landscape of the soul. Should one maintain oneself on the threshold between day consciousness and sleep, image formations will project on the screen of the psyche expressing our attunements or moods, perhaps even premonitions and misgivings in a pictorial form. This ability is cultivated by the Sufis.

Hence the meditation techniques fostered by the Sufis which gave rise to visionary narratives such as those of Shihabuddin Suhrawardhi, Ibn 'Arabi, Najm ud Din Kubra, Abd el Karim al Jili, elucidated by Prophet Mohammed's recount of his visit of the heavenly spheres (in the Miraj).

Rather like the paintings of the impressionists, (though these are dynamic), the landscapes of the soul thus projected by our creative imagination may be reminiscent of familiar physical landscapes though varying from realistic nature scenes to transfigured soul-scapes fashioned in light and traversed with a diaphanous glow. While the landscapes thus spirited may give us a clue about our perception of our relationship with the current psychological environment or situation, the features of our effigy, chiseled in light, curiously enough being of a similar fabric to the envisioned environment, are more likely to give us a clue about our personal make-up. Our dream image is a cross between our transpersonal self and our 'persona', that is the peripheral area of our psyche that adapts itself to circumstance, whereas the environment of our reverie is a projection of our rapport with the environment. Conversely the environment rubs off on our own effigy perceived as our personal identity.

Thus the information culled in the state of reverie will give us information about the osmosis between ourselves and the psychological environment that escapes the scrutiny of our conscious observation and therefore proves invaluable.

Moreover, we enjoy a curious leverage on our self-transformation at the threshold of the unconscious, not by dint of volitional intervention (which is not the way that creativity works), but by simply giving vent to a paradoxical attunement whereby the cosmic dimensions of our emotions supersede the more personal dimensions of our emotion. Our very built-in programming does this better than what we could achieve by our will, exactly as in the case of the great composers and artists. This is why Christ and in fact all mystics say "Thy will rather than my will". In fact, in the holistic perspective: the divine will is the transcendental dimension of our will and our will is the personal dimension of the divine will.

"The difference between the divine and the human will is like the difference between the trunk of a tree and its branches."[51]

"Divinity is human perfection and humanity is divine limitation." Hazrat Inayat Khan[52]

Pir Vilayat Inayat-Khan is an internationally known lecturer at seminars and conferences or symposia where he interfaces the methods of meditation of the esoteric schools of the world religions with current views in psychology and science and he illustrates the experience with classical and sacred music.

He applies the know-how gained by incorporating these wide fields in the course of retreats in Europe, U.S.A., sometimes India. He leads with a view to sharpening the participant's perspicacity, so as to foster their self creativity, particularly facing human problems.

---

[51] From lecture notes.
[52] Gayan, Vadan & Nirtan, Sufi Order Publications, Lebanon Springs, N.Y. 1980, p. 28.

Pir Vilayat is the successor of Hazrat Pir-o-Murshid Inayat Khan of the lineage of the Chisti Order, Ajmer, India, the first Sufi master to introduce Sufism to the West (in 1910).

Pir Vilayat was born in London, his mother was American, a cousin of Mrs Eddie Baker and niece of Theos Bernard. He is resident in France, but travels extensively. He has a master's degree in Psychology from the Sorbonne and pursued additional studies in Oxford. He trained in the school of the Chisti Sufis of India and in addition carried out retreats in the caves of the Himalayas, amongst the Buddhists and in Christian monasteries. He is the author of **Towards the One, A Message in Our Time** (published by Harper and Row), **The Spiritual Dimension of Counseling, The Call of the Dervish** (published by Omega Press), **A Sequential Course in Meditation** and several articles.

Interviewed, Pir Vilayat tells us how he underwent a crisis in his life at university, studying philosophy and science which he had difficulty in integrating with his spiritual background and it was Bergson and Jung who provided him with a bridge which he then explored further.

The Art of Spiritual Guidance

By Atum O'Kane

The Guide: A Mirror of the Self

The spiritual guide functions in the Sufi Order in the West as a facilitator in awakening the initiate to the transpersonal dimension. The role of the guide functions on the archetypal sphere and in the realm of the human personality. The guide is a bridge by which the initiate is able to cross into the transpersonal realm and integrate dimensions discovered there into the fabric of his/her individual personality and life.

Carl Jung commented, "Mystical experience is experience of archetypes." (Walsh-Vaughan, 1980, p. 82.) The spiritual guide in the Sufi Order is one who has travelled the archetypal landscape, using the maps left by previous explorers, but who is not blindly following in their footsteps. What the guide can offer to seekers who want to discover the transpersonal or mystical dimension, is an understanding of its topography and a willingness to travel with the seeker, offering assistance drawn from experience and intuition.

The archetypes of the spiritual teacher and student, and the patterns of their relationship, find expression in a wide variety of religious literature, from the dialogue of the teacher and the disciple in the Upanishads to the Hassidic teaching, Zen tales, the Journals of Thomas Merton, and Sufi tales. Each may have a flavoring of its own particular mystical tradition, but they are united in a common archetypical pattern.

> "The archetypes provide patterns of meaning and guides to growth for the developing personality. A person's conscious experience is what gives an archetype specific content. Archetypes cannot be known in themselves. They are nucleii of a complex, drawing associated material from an individual's experience to themselves." (Welch, 19821, p. 73.)

The above quote is taken from **Spiritual Pilgrims**, a wonderful book by John Welch, which examines the mystical journeys of Teresa of Avila and Carl Jung. I have included the quote because it conveys the major thrust of the role of the spiritual guide as I see it. The student experiences in the teacher the reflection of the archetype of the self which provides patterns of meaning and guides to growth for the developing personality of the pupil. Since the archetype cannot be known in itself, associated material is drawn from the one who personifies the teacher, thereby giving the archetype specific content.

From the perspective of the Sufi Order in the West, the purpose of this relationship is to lead the student to Self-realization. In the words of Hazrat Inayat Khan,

"It is in Self-realization that the mystery of the whole of life is centered. It is the remedy of all maladies, it is the secret of success in all walks of life, it is a religion and more than a religion. What is wrong with humanity today is that it is not itself and all the misery of the world is caused by this. Therefore, nothing can answer the need of humanity save this process of the sages and wise of all ages, which leads some to Self-realization." (Khan, H.I., 1985, p. 30)

Self can also be understood in the light of Jung's use of the word. "Self, a term on the one hand, definite enough to convey the essence of human wholeness and on the other hand, infinite enough to express the indescribable and indeterminable nature of this wholeness." (Welch, 1982, p. 192) "The Self may be called the God within us and all our highest and ultimate purposes seem to be striving towards it." (Jung, 1956, p. 22)

Jolande Jacobi (1974), in **Complex, Archetypes, Symbol in the Psychology of C. G. Jung,** offers this insight into the archetype of the self. "The Self is also a point of departure, the fertile soil from which all future life will spring. This premonition of futurity is as clearly impressed upon our innermost feelings as is the historical aspect." (p. 65) The phenomenon of growth in the initiate of the Sufi Order, facilitated through his/her relationship with the spiritual guide, can be translated into the lens of transpersonal psychology by adopting the terms of Jungian psychology. The archetype of the Self is projected upon the teacher which enables the student to grow in Self-realization or the process of individuation. Because the Self has the "premonition of futurity," the students recognize in the teacher their future growth, unfoldment, next step. Since the archetype of the Self is never fully known, it may continuously reveal new aspects reflected in the teacher. The visionary nature of this unique relationship and its capacity for transformation are its special gifts.

There is a story which Pir Vilayat tells from his own experience that captures the essential role of the teacher. While a young man, he set forth on his first trip to India in search of dervishes, rishis, and other "great beings." He had heard many stories about them in his father's teachings and longed to meet them "in the flesh." Eventually, he made his way to the region which his father had said was the abode of the holiest being. The young Vilayat discovered a being who filled his deepest yearnings. At the moment of their encounter, the rishi asked him, "Why have you come so far to see yourself?" Some time later, Pir Vilayat realized the answer to the rishi's question: "I had to see what I could be before I could become it."

The spiritual teacher offers a vision of how the archetype of the Self can manifest. In the terminology of the Sufi Order in the West, one would say that the teacher acts as a reflection of one's own eternal being, face, or soul. Pir Vilayat speaks of life as a continuous process of Self-discovery. The spiritual teacher is a catalyst for discovering the potential Self that has been sensed, but not articulated within one.

In my own initial encounter with Pir Vilayat, the element of Self-discovery was crucial. From the time of my childhood, I remember knowing that people held the promise of becoming exquisite beings of unlimited richness, yet I never encountered anyone in whom I recognized the expression of that possibility. Later, I realized that the missing aspect was the development of the transpersonal dimension of the human being. I had reached the point of having to consider that my "vision" was not to be realized or was not real. In meeting Pir Vilayat for the first time, I recognized the conscious development of the transpersonal dimension in a human being. My reason for studying with him is that he seeks to share all he has discovered and therefore, I felt that the richness in him can also be evoked in me.

My relationship with Pir Vilayat is a retelling of his encounter with the rishi who asked, "Why have you come so far to see yourself?" I would also answer, "I need to see my Self, in order to become the Self" which of course is a continuous process.

There are many authentic spiritual teachers, but my relationship with Pir Vilayat has been profound because his particular mode of being resonates with similar qualities in me. From my experience as a student and spiritual guide, I am aware that the recognition of yourself in the teacher is essential. From others, you may receive insight, support and assistance in unfolding your potential, but the "vision of your soul" manifested in the teacher is unique, traumatic and compelling.

The following quote from Hazrat Inayat Khan (1985) captures this point beautifully. "What is it that the initiator teaches the initiated one? He tells the initiated one the truth of his own being. He does not tell him something new or different. He tells him something which his soul already knows but which his mind has forgotten." (p. 12)

The Vision Carrier

"To make a dream come true, one must have a dream, believe in it, and work toward it. Often it is essential that another significant person believes that dream is possible; that person is a vision carrier whose faith is crucial." (Bolen, 1984, p. 29) The description of the spiritual guide as a "vision carrier" is most fitting, for it captures one of the major functions of the teacher. The spiritual guide believes in your dream or vision of yourself and is able to reflect it back to you in a way that empowers it and articulates its detail. His or her faith in you and your vision, which are essentially linked, becomes the catalyst to sustain the vision through periods of doubt, and lifts you beyond your lack of confidence. "I think the vision carrier — therapist, mentor, teacher or parent with a 'green thumb,' under whom others bloom and develop their gifts — evokes what research psychologist Robert Rosenthal named the 'Pygmalion effect.' This term describes the power of positive expectation on the behavior of others." (Bolen, 1984, p. 231)

The above quote contained in **Goddesses in Everywoman**, by Jean Bolen, conveys the transforming effect of the teacher upon the student. She expounds upon this theme when speaking of the role of a "special woman" in the transition stage of a young man into the adult sphere. Drawing upon the work of Daniel Levinson in **Seasons of a Man's Life**, she offers the following comment upon the function of this kind of vision carrier. "She helps him to shape and live out the dream. She shares it, believes in him as its hero, gives it her blessing, joins him on the journey, and provides a sanctuary where his aspirations can be imagined and his hopes nourished." (Bolen, 1984, p. 230)

The qualities enumerated in the "special woman" are fundamental to the function of the spiritual guide. As mentioned in the opening of this section, my initial attraction to Pir Vilayat stemmed from recognizing in him the awareness of a vision long held within me that centered on the transpersonal potential of the human being. He shared that vision which was expressed in his teachings and vividly saw it in me. Through the spiritual guidance and practices he has shared with me, that inner dream has moved into partial manifestation. He has indeed provided a sanctuary from a world which denied the transpersonal dimension of the human being which was so essential to my dream, and he has nourished my hope through his example and faith in me. We have joined together on the journey which is beautifully reflected in Pir Vilayat's favorite metaphor for the relationship of the spiritual guide and student. He describes a mountain climbing venture in which the experienced climber assists the novice through certain passages, drawing upon the guide's past experience of finding his/her way through the landscape.

In describing the special woman as a vision carrier, the phrase, "gives it her blessing" was used. This quality seems especially significant for the spiritual teacher. I remember that "blessing" which I received from Pir Vilayat as he functioned as my vision carrier. I experience it now as an infusion of life within me, stemming from my teacher's affirmation of my vision. A blessing is more than support, for in it I feel the teacher's spirit join with mine, giving a new life and presence that carries me beyond the doubt of my personality. This has also been my experience when functioning as a spiritual guide to others and in carrying on the role of vision carrier which I learned with Pir Vilayat.

There is a great potential for psychological and spiritual injury to the student if the teacher is not able to fulfill the role of vision carrier or if he or she uses the role to foster the student's dependency in order to satisfy personal needs or gratification. Hazrat Inayat Khan offered the following warning: "It is well to remember that such utter trust should never be reposited in the teacher until the Self has gained entire confidence in him and every doubt has been subdued." (Khan, H.I., 1985, p. 12)

Breaking the Idol

Pir Vilayat has answered questions concerning the authenticity of a spiritual guide by warning that no one has the right to ask something of you that goes against your conscience. He also advises not to evaluate another's spiritual evolution by their words and actions alone, but by their atmosphere (which cannot be manipulated). The guide must also be continuously aware of the danger of a student who has unrealistic expectations of the guide. There is a tendency found in some of the literature, stories and customs of various traditions which accents the positive archetypical dimension of the spiritual teacher while not fully recognizing that the person is functioning in a role. However, the guide is a human being and the Sufi Order in the West embraces that humanness, rather than denies or shuns it. "As he [the guide] is just another human being, he is limited, exactly as the pupil is; he is as liable to make mistakes and to have failures as anyone. He enjoys no special authority nor is he one who stands apart in holiness." (Khan, H.I., 1985, p. 12)

If students and guides were to continuously review the above statement by Hazrat Inayat Khan, it would help prevent feelings of disillusion, betrayal and rejection when the teacher is revealed as a human being and not just the projection of an archetype. Guides would also be encouraged to accept their humanness and would not be burdened with the tendency to suppress or deny facets of their personality.

From my own experience, there is a feeling of gnawing hollowness within when one is not being authentic while engaged in the role of the spiritual guide. Students can strongly desire that you only interact with them in accordance with the way they want to see you. This can lead to an artificial performance by the guide. At this stage, the words of the Sufi Master, Jelaluddin Rumi, often quoted by Pir Vilayat, strike the note of truth which breaks the facade: "The teacher must shatter the idol which others make of him/her." (Khan, P.V., 1984, p. 454) This note is especially important in Sufism which stresses that only God is to be worshipped. "The real teacher is in the heart of the person. The outward teacher is only a sign." (Khan, H.I., 1985, p. 21) A sign points the way but is not the purpose or end of the path.

There is something powerful and appealing for both parties when the pupil looks upon the guide with the eyes of a worshipper toward an idol. For the guide, the danger lies in not realizing that the life and meaning of the idol are dependent upon the worshipper. The student who turns the guide into an idol sacrifices the possibility of experiencing a full human relationship and focuses upon the idol rather than seeing the teacher as a reflection of his or her own soul.

How does the guide break the idol which has been created through misdirected devotion or a misunderstanding of the role of the guide? One way is by not playing into expectations; another is by puncturing the inflated picture made of the guide by maintaining a commitment to authenticity. This is a difficult task when one is faced repeatedly with the appealing glow which surrounds the glance of the devotee. The idol must be shattered continuously, but with care taken not to destroy the student's faith in the growth which can arise from this relationship. As Hazrat Inayat Khan wisely observed, "It is not enough to know the truth; one has to know human psychology in order to impart the truth." (Khan, H.I., 1978, p. 10) If the idol is not broken by the teacher, the day will come when even a mundane incident can shatter the spell. In a conversation with Frances Vaughan, former President of the Transpersonal Psychology Association, she wisely noted that if people have raised one to infatuated heights, they will some day drop you with equal intensity. This observation resonates with Hazrat Inayat Khan's comment, "The message of today is balance." (Khan, H.I., 1978, p. 97)

The art of functioning as a spiritual guide is extremely subtle and demands the balancing of opposites. The guide must seek authenticity in the relationship by remembering his or her own humanness and yet honor the archetypical vision of the Self which the student finds reflected in the guide. This topic was touched upon in an interview with Reb Zalman Schachter, Professor of the Psychology of Religion at Temple University. In responding to my questions about the role of the spiritual teacher, he drew upon his experience as a teacher of Jewish mysticism and commented upon the ease among the younger generations of spiritual guides in putting on and taking off the role.

"That next echelon is so talented; that's what I'm so excited about. How talented the people are and how they put on the role and take off the role. They're not always in the role of the teacher. Whereas the previous teachers have been set apart by their setup, the way in which they work with people is the old kingly model. In that position, they have done their thing all the time instead of taking off the cloak, as it were." (O'Kane, A. 1985, p. 4)

The ability to "put on and take off the role" implies knowing the function, limits and appropriateness of the role of the spiritual guide, rather than assuming it as one's total identity. This ability accents the nature of role as one of functional attunement rather than of being a superior archetype. In the Sufi Order, the spiritual guide is not viewed as necessarily more evolved or illuminated than the student. He or she is one equipped with a deeper understanding of the teachings and spiritual practices used by the Order. These practices are used to awaken the promise of divinity contained in the human being through a process of God-realization and Self-realization. This view is reflected in the words of Hazrat Inayat Khan: "Although the outer form may appear to be hierarchy, yet the Sufi message leads to true democracy for it holds the promise of that goal which is the yearning of every soul." (Khan, H.I., 1985, p. 16)

The Teacher as Pupil

The danger for the teacher is in thinking, "I have got it." Whether the "it" is enlightenment, self actualization, individuation or God-consciousness, the role is not a fixed position obtained by a Divine certification program. Pir Vilayat describes realization as the horizon which is ever receding as one advances. The questions and issues raised by the student are a source of growth for the teacher. However, the growth can only occur if the person in the role does not view him/herself as having to be omnipotent.

It has been my experience as a guide that the issues a student is dealing with are paramount in my own life. In working toward some insight, we are a catalyst for each other. I can only grow from the realization these issues help to facilitate in me if I see myself as a perpetual learner. "It is easy to become a teacher, but difficult to become a pupil. The lesson we all have to learn is that of discipleship. It is the first and last lesson." (Khan, H.I., 1985, p. 14)

A way to detect the authenticity of spiritual teachers is by their willingness to state that they do not know "the answer." Out of the fear of losing face or revealing inadequacy, guides may attempt to conceal their ignorance with an evasive "mystical" response, implying that it is a paradoxical koan. Here, an authentic teaching method is being distorted and the role is manipulated to shield the teacher's inflated, yet vulnerable ego. During Hazrat Inayat Khan's life, a group of students selected a representative to ask him if he could make a mistake. He responded with immediate laughter and commented that if he didn't make mistakes, he couldn't be able to teach anything for his mistakes were the source of his wisdom.

When viewed in a narrow manner, the "teacher" can be seen as a stagnant position of complete knowledge and authority. This, of course, ends the possibility of further realization of the one in that role. If the spiritual guide is viewed as an eternal pupil who shares evolving realization with those newer to the realms of his/her awareness, then the role is a more dynamic, growing, transforming one. In being true to his/her path of spiritual growth, the teacher may be called to enter a stage or experience which does not resonate with the pupil's, or may even repulse the other. The teacher is tested at that moment whether to follow an internal yearning or affirm the security and comfort of the student at the sacrifice of the teacher's own growth.

Pir Vilayat, commenting on this dilemma, has noted that people often come to study with him while he is in a particular station. When the vitality of his soul casts its glance in another direction, students may withdraw from the relationship. Still, Pir must follow what is living for him since it is not just information which he is sharing but the communication of an attunement or state of being. He has commented that his own awareness of the transpersonal dimension has not been gained by following various meditation instructions but by being able to meditate with highly attuned beings who lifted him into their state of consciousness.

My own experience of this issue centers on periods when I have been immersed in a certain attunement or station which found expression in the classes, seminars, retreats, and spiritual guidance that I was sharing. Those seeking the same attunement were drawn because it resonated with a parallel state in their growth. I vividly remember sensing a shift in my being to a new attunement. As I began to lead a seminar, the atmosphere was filled with the expectation that we would touch the quality which had been the signature of my work at that time. There was no movement within me toward that state at that particular moment but I felt my being thrust in a new direction. At that moment, I felt a similarity to those popular singers destined to continue performing their old hits and afraid to risk new material for fear of losing their reliable audience.

A Special Friendship

There is another aspect which I believe is essential for the one who functions in the role of spiritual guide, and it is conveyed in the following rendering of my initial encounter with Pir Vilayat. Our meeting occurred against the dramatic background of an inter-religious camp which he had convened at 8,000 feet in the French Alps, across from Mont Blanc. When I first took the cable car up to the campsite, there was another young man who had just arrived. We spoke about what had drawn us to this gathering, as the cable car lifted us higher and higher. The houses and buildings associated with the daily routine of life disappeared below. As we walked to the camp, a surprising settlement of large white Arabian-looking tents, we touched upon our mutual search for a spiritual teacher. There was the romance of the "guru search" associated with the counter culture movement that flowered in the sixties. Neither of us was quite sure what it was that we were seeking, but the quest was an earnest one. My only guidance was contained in the parting words of a former yoga teacher who advised me that when I met my teacher, my heart would know him/her. This, of course, was compatible with the mystery of the journey and as it turned out, a very wise insight.

During the two weeks of the camp, we "checked out" the various teachers: a Hindu Swami, a Tibetan Lama, an Alchemist, and of course, Pir Vilayat. Periodically, we would come together and compare notes; my friend was aware of a growing bond between Pir Vilayat and me. One morning, we met after breakfast and my companion informed me that he was leaving for India to continue his search. He asked me if I had found my teacher in Pir Vilayat. After some soul searching, I responded that I didn't know if Pir was my teacher, but he had become the best friend I had ever known. My answer was surprising to me.

After the parting, I attended Pir Vilayat's morning meditation and heard him describe the spiritual teacher as one's "best friend." The words thrust open the doors of my heart and my whole being resonated with recognition. The following words of Hazrat Inayat Khan describe the potential contained in this special bond. "This friendship, this relationship which is initiated by two people, is something which cannot be broken; it is something which cannot be separated; it is something which cannot be compared with anything else in the world. It belongs to eternity." (Khan, H.I., 1985, p. 11) The hallmark of this relationship is trust. The student knows there is someone with whom he/she can reveal his/her "darkest secrets" or shadow, and this will not diminish the love the teacher holds for him or her, or mar the vision of their eternal being held firm by the guide. My testing of this special friendship was immediate. During my initial meeting with Pir Vilayat, I volunteered for a *darshan* session. Pir led all those attending the camp in a meditation, and then shared his vision of my eternal being. He articulated a deep felt reality within me that had never been recognized by anyone before, or so vividly comprehended by me.

The session was both exalting and traumatic. Having been "seen" in such a manner, I became afraid that Pir would then discover dimensions of my being that were not so beautiful and yet all too familiar to me. I began to hide when there was an occasion for a personal encounter. I tried desperately to live up to that positive vision and repress other parts of me. Finally, the strain pushed me to the point of realizing that if Pir Vilayat was unable to retain his love and vision of me in face of my imperfections, then the relationship was not one of a spiritual guide and seeker. I also realized that if his vision was keen enough to see the light of my soul, then he must be aware of the shadows of my personality. Attempting a facade was a ridiculous game.

As my spiritual training evolved, I shared with Pir Vilayat my "darkest secrets," for meeting them is a key to spiritual growth. He has always responded with a love that encourages openness, a lack of judgment which helps me to reevaluate my own opinions about the issues, and a reaffirmation of the vision which he sees in my soul. Because my personal experience in this area has been so transforming, the aspect of friendship has become a primary focus in my work as a spiritual guide.

For several years, I have worked with a member of the Sufi Order in a unique relationship. In another guide, this initiate sees a reflection of her soul which she describes as detached, impersonal, immaculate, aloof, beyond the beyond, Buddha-like. However, the very qualities described prevent her from feeling the warmth and acceptance of unconditional friendship which she finds reflected in me. This friendship allows her to share her "negative" aspects and discover in them the power of transformation and growth. For years she has tried to force herself to make a choice between the two guides, although we guides have never thought it necessary. Recently, she realized that both vision and friendship are essential parts of this process and one cannot be sacrificed for the other. This experience further confirms my belief that vision and friendship are fundamental components which teachers must bring to their work.

Pir Vilayat's reflections capture the spirit of this uniquely wonderful relationship. "As the pupil advances, the relationship with the teacher becomes more and more wonderful; it is a mutual and tacit understanding beyond words. It culminates in the most perfect friendship." (Khan, P.V., 1978, p. 380)

"The position of the teacher toward the pupil is very delicate. He should be closely attached and yet detached, near and yet far." (Khan, H.I. — Khan, P.V., 1978, p. 27) This quote from Hazrat Inayat Khan on the art of guiding initiates strikes at the heart of a very difficult balance. The guide has been spoken of as the closest friend, which means there must be a very intimate bond of love, yet Pir Vilayat has also cautioned that moving the relationship into the realm of "chums" can break the thread which unites the initiate and initiator because the sacred will be reduced to the profane. This can lead to a loss of respect for the teacher and he/she may no longer be able to function as a vision carrier.

In an interview, Elaine Resnick, a psychotherapist and Sufi Order Guide, affirmed the need for a clearly structured interaction with students similar to those used in psychotherapy. The interview concerned the issue of transference in the relationship between the guide and student.

"Structuring sessions or interviews is also highly important. There's a clear structure, for example, for seeing the patients in psychotherapy that's based on developmental psychology. The time limits for sessions are defined. Meetings take place in one place without interruptions and the therapist should expect nothing from the client except payment for the time. The purpose of these structured parameters is to limit transference distortions, so that the likelihood of being able to explore and deal with transference issues is increased. Perhaps the rigidity of some of these parameters can be questioned, but many are essential for effective treatment." (O'Kane, A., 1985, p.4)

Other members of the Order have felt that this kind of structure is unnatural because it doesn't allow for spontaneous interaction. The student is unable to observe the guide in a variety of situations and learn from his/her responses. At a gathering of guides several years ago, some expressed their sense of isolation in the role. I believe the balance between "attachment and detachment, near and far" in this relationship is one that each guide must determine in accordance with his/her temperament, experience and effectiveness in the role and the particular dynamic of each student. I know effective guides at either end of the scale. This issue is also related to the guide's ability to put on and take off the role.

From my experience and observation, the more mature the guide and the student are in the process, the better able they are to assume a variety of ways of relating according to the appropriateness of the occasion.

Retreats: The Alchemical Process

We shall understand the world when we understand ourselves: for it and we are inseparable halves of one whole. We are children of God, divine seeds. One day, we shall be what our Father is. (DeRola, S., 1982)

Pir Vilayat has developed a formula for personal transformation conducted in a retreat format under the supervision of a trained guide, which seeks to promote the retreatant's realization of the divine seeds which are the core of his/her being. The six stages contained in the process are drawn from the teachings of the alchemists and apply to the disintegration and re-creation of the human personality. The various stages are contained in the fundamental structure of all life but are not usually observed, for we tend to be absorbed in the demands of the moment. The retreat offers a concentrated period when one can consciously participate in the alchemical process, seeking to promote a breakthrough in realization and transformation. Perhaps its most creative function is opening the doors to the next step in one's unfoldment. In the course of this section we shall examine the six stages in the alchemical process, for they are valuable to the guide in helping to understand how the personality is continuously disintegrating in order to rebuild. The material contained in the first half of this section, relating to Pir Vilayat's teachings on the six stages, was originally part of my Master's thesis (completed in 1981) and is presented with minor modifications. This teaching and its application in the Sufi Order training continues to be essentially the same. The latter part of this section which draws parallels between the alchemical teachings presented here and Murray Stein's Jungian approach to mid-life has been created for this study.

The Sufi Order uses the principles and related meditation practices of the alchemical process for transformation in both spiritual counseling and retreats. The purpose of the stages is to provide a framework for growth in which a person is constantly incorporating more and more of his/her eternal archetype and the totality into one's personality.

> The overall schedule is based upon the stages in the process of transformation outlined in *Ars Regia*, the royal art of the alchemist. This method was used by the Sufis, who were among the first alchemists, outlined by Valentinus, and has been referred to in our time by Carl Jung. (Khan, P.V., 1979, p. 9)

The first three stages are concerned with dissolving the transient aspects of one's being in order to identify the essentials. The alchemist refers to the first half of the process as the lunar phase or minor mysteries. The focus is to make apparent the various illusions in our perception of life and ourselves. However, Pir Vilayat warns that our illusions are nature's protection for we realize the degree of the truth which we are capable of integrating. The guide must be very careful in seeking to dispel a student's illusions, for the personality may be over-whelmed and shattered when faced with the truth. The foundation for a new personality structure, capable of handling such intense changes, must have been constructed before such an encounter.

To foster the first stage, a student can be assigned meditation practices which focus on recalling events of his or her life. The suggestion of viewing the flow of one's life as a film can be given, for it evokes a degree of dis-identification which creates greater objectivity. The purpose is in marking the interrelationship between one's personality and the events in one's life. Events have shaped one's personality in a certain form but one's personality has also influenced and created the events in one's life.

Causal connections may become apparent which normally would not be noticed. In viewing our life as a film, the focus of the sequences and the interconnections in the life's script are drawn to our attention. Consciousness is expanded beyond the here and now.

Stage One

The essence of stage one seeks a change in the definition of oneself. The guide assists the initiate in realizing that one's personality is not a fixed entity but that it must, by nature, be continuously changing if growth is to occur. The meditation on viewing one's life as a film raises the question: What is the constant or core of one's being in the midst of a constantly changing personality?

Since the personality is an expression of the notion of the self, the personality undergoes change. It must necessarily do so, just as the body does. One has to learn to transfer one's notion of oneself from the fixed image one has acquired to the notion of being a continuity in change, a current rather than an entity. (Khan, P.V., 1979, p.7)

Stage Two

The second stage consists in disidentifying oneself from everything that is subject to becoming and decay. By identifying the eternal archetype of one's being, one salvages that which survives death and disintegration. (Khan, P.V., 1979, p.8)

This shift from identifying with the personality to identifying with the eternal archetype, occurs through a movement of consciousness from the individual perspective to the transpersonal dimension. Meditation practices are given to discriminate the essential elements of one's being which are always present in the core as compared to attitudes, impressions and aspects which have been adopted for a period of time. The personality is experienced as the limited exemplar of one's eternal archetype.

Better still, one can identify with the archetype of one's personality. One discovers oneself as always having existed as a particular blend of qualities, and thus one is able to observe the personality one assumes in one's present existence as an offshoot of one's root... (Khan, P.V., 1979, p. 8)

Stage Three

The third stage completes the movement of consciousness from the personal to the transpersonal and unity dimensions in a vertical continuity. In the various phases of the ascent, one has discovered oneself to be consciousness, intelligence, and the life force, and finally pure spirit.

One remembers having had a body that is located somewhere on the planet, and one used to be able to use one's mind to channel thought, but this now seems like a hoax. Logic seems to be a framework for consciousness trapped in its focus in the notion of the self, limiting understanding, whereas one intuits transcendental logic such as that referred to by Ouspensky in the **New Model of the Universe**. (Khan, P.V., 1979, p. 12)

The condition described in the above quotation by Pir Vilayat represents the state of a person in the third stage of the alchemical process when the whole personality has dissolved. This is experienced in meditations that promote *Samadhi*, dissolving one's sense of individuality and returning to a state beyond all forms as in deep sleep. The purpose in descending from *Samadhi* back into individuality is that personality can be re-created. The last three stages are concerned with this reintegration of the personality.

The absorption of one into a state of *Samadhi* or pure spirit simultaneously dissolves the focalized elements of the personality structure while initiating a new dispensation of life. Both the mystic who has sought this encounter, through dissolving individual identity, and the schizophrenic touch the same dimension. Pir Vilayat notes that the difference is the mystic can integrate the experience while the schizophrenic does not complete the next three stages in the process. In the latter case, the old personality structure has dispersed, usually because it faced a situation beyond its scope, and a new one is not being created.

Then one experiences oneself as life force, not *a* life force, and beyond life force, pure spirit; the life of life, as the Sufis say, or we could say the catalyst of incipient life. In addition, spirit is envisioned as the thrust which breaks the sclerosis which sets in when life forces crisscross, stalemate, and become cyclic. (Khan, P.V., 1979, p. 9)

Stage Four

An image which conveys something of this alchemical process is a clay statue. The artist, filled with inspiration, creates a statue out of clay in order to give expression to a creative impulse which surges inside. Initially, the artist is pleased with the work, for it represents an understanding of the inspiration combined with creative talents. Later, the artist grows dissatisfied with the work, sensing it is not complete. A new insight occurs, revealing a deeper meaning in the original inspiration which manifests in the vision of a clay statue far richer than the first. The artist dissolves the form of the first statue, returning the clay to its original ball shape, and then proceeds to rework the same clay into a new and greater statue.

Our personality is like the clay and is continuously being formed into a structure that gives expression to some of the potential contained in our eternal archetype. Once the personality becomes locked into a certain pattern, it becomes fossilized. In this process, growth comes from disidentification with the personality and discovering the deeper non-individual identity of unity consciousness and that is the purpose of the first three stages in the alchemical process. The last three stages are concerned with rearranging elements of the personality and awakening latent potential, so the new personality structure embodies more of the richness contained in one's eternal archetype.

The fourth stage is one of rebirth, when a person "proceeds to rebuild his personality intentionally and consciously, participating in all phases of his/her own recreation." (Khan, P.V., 1979, p. 12) Often people feel they have been shaped by influences and events far beyond their control so the opportunity to be consciously involved in the creation of one's personality is very profound. Certain meditation themes are given to help a person realize the richness and vastness which lie dormant in his or her nature. They mark the conception of a new personality.

> The subject is made to earmark the qualities he inherits from his father and mother, resolving conflicts that may have existed between them. Then he includes ancestors, wherever known, envisioned as numberless strands that have become intertwined, nay interfused, into his being. This includes inheritance from the animal, vegetable and mineral realms,

and inheritances from the djinn and angelic spheres and from all planes, and finally the divine inheritance. These are attributes we previously acquired as eternal archetypes before we co-opted the substance of the different planes in our descent. (Khan, P.V., 1979, p. 13)

This stage is essential in counseling someone whose life has been completely shattered. One meets people whose personality structures are dependent upon a certain lifestyle or relationships. Any sudden change in these and the personality structure breaks down, for it cannot cope with the new demands of life. The perspective from which reality was interpreted and dealt with has been lost. To these people this change may appear as a great tragedy and they will desperately try to re-create the past, for they are without a foundation. The counselor must help them to move forward, which often means completing the breakdown of the old structure so a new one can emerge. According to this approach, life is progressive and such incidents, although they seem at the moment to be a great loss, can serve the purpose of promoting new growth. The elements in stage four can help a person caught in the pain and depression of such shatterings turn the corner. It is a stage of great creativity and begins to awaken in one a new enthusiasm for life and the vast potential in oneself.

Stage Five

The focus of this stage is centered upon incorporating archetypes and qualities into one's personality. One meditates upon the spectrum of attributes which, in various combinations, are embodied in the universe and latent in one's eternal archetype. For example, while contemplating the power that moves the universe, you awaken that same power in yourself. The use of *mantra* or *wazifa* promotes the embodiment of a quality in the personality by repeating the sounds which correspond with its vibrational frequency.

Perhaps the most valuable meditation in this vein is that of entering into the consciousness of a great human being who manifests a particular quality to a high degree of perfection. The quality ceases to be an abstraction and one discovers how it can function in a person. The blending of two opposite qualities is very difficult, but can be experienced by meditating upon the sovereignty and humility found in Christ or the combination of detachment and compassion present in Buddha. Reflecting the lives of such beings shows how these qualities functioned in very concrete situations, and can be related to the problems one faces. In each archetype is embodied the realization of certain attitudes and each quality has a representative archetype. The key meditation in stage five is that of the Ideal Being. Creative imagination inspired by one's longing for an ideal forms a being in whom one can discover one's vision of perfection in human form.

A practice borrowed from the East consists in representing oneself as sitting in front of an ideal person — the guru image of one's most utopian daydreaming — and gradually identifying with him until one realizes that one could not have imagined him if one did not have his ideosyncrasies embedded in one's own psyche. It is easier to see oneself in another self who can manifest what one is better than one can oneself. (Khan, P.V., 1979, p. 13)

The conception of a new personality which occurs in the previous stage is made more concrete in stage five. Contemplating a spectrum of qualities and archetypes will bring to life those attributes which were latent in the person. Perhaps qualities which were secondary before will become dominant and vice versa, because their ordering will be based upon one's eternal archetype and not a response to past conditioning. "In the fifth stage the candidate has to learn to identify with his new image and resist the influences of friends who tend to force him back into the image that they have become used to." (Khan, P.V., 1979, p. 13)

Stage Six

With a new personality synthesized, one enters into the midst of life. A new perspective enriches one's understanding while newly discovered qualities and talents await expression. It is important to act upon all the richness which has emerged during the alchemical process while inspiration is still fresh and energy high. If one waits, circumstances often draw one into past patterns and the new realizations fade.

One must hold to the remembrance that one's personal perspective is limited and must be complemented by lifting consciousness into the higher and vaster dimensions which meditation promotes.

Returning to life in the sixth stage, the meditator is now equipped with insight gained at high altitudes and is expected to resist the tendency to slip back into his personal vantage point. He is therefore supposed to maintain the supreme perspective while involved in life. (Khan, P.V., 1979, p. 14)

This perspective must be combined with an awareness of the richness contained in one's being. The remembrance of one's eternal archetype and the fullness of one's nature becomes a source of inspiration when limitations press upon one. The infusion of pure spirit experienced in stage three will continue to act as a catalyst for changing old patterns while releasing a new dispensation of the life force. Having completed the process, one carries dimensions from all of the stages now integrated in one's being and enacted in one's life.

The Seventh Stage

In the summer of 1980, Pir Vilayat began to speak about a new stage which he called "resurrection." The first six stages form a cycle that continuously repeats itself as life moves in a horizontal direction from past to future. This is the forward movement of evolution. The seventh stage is vertical with a movement upward, as that which has been eternalized out of the unfoldment of life is resurrected. Here we are concerned with what is gained by existence. What is the ultimate value of our lives to the Universe, God, and us?

If we refer back to the comparison of the human being and the seed, we can understand this stage. It takes the unfoldment of ten thousand roses to make one pound of rose oil. Even though the petals quickly fade, the essence of their beauty lives on in the rose oil. The events and relationships in our lives fade with the passing of time, but the wisdom they have produced lives on. In this stage, one identifies how the seed of one's eternal archetype has been enriched through its unfoldment in the process of life. What has been resurrected from the death of continuous change? One may even ask what has God gained through my living? It is a search for the essence, the rose oil of our being, which shall survive the petal-like formations of our personality.

The alchemical process used by Pir Vilayat reveals seven stages of a human growth cycle which assist the guide in better understanding a student's perspective, emotions and life situations and placing them in a framework that gives the guide the advantage of an overview. Then the teacher can work in assisting the student to make the full transition from one stage to the next. This model of transformation and growth has the richness of including transpersonal dimensions of the human being but like any model it is an incomplete rendering of the richness and mystery of the human experience and should not be rigidly conformed to as an absolute map of reality.

The spiritual foundation of the alchemical process is the vision of life as the materialization of spirit and the spiritualization of matter.

This is referred to as the alchemical marriage which finds its most perfect union in the human being.

Parallels in Jungian Psychology

My own entrance into the mid-life passage has led me to seek out persons and books which shed some light upon this transition time. One of the most important discourses I have encountered is Jungian analyst Murray Stein's **In Midlife**, and part of my interest stems from parallels found in his work and the alchemical process as it is used in the Sufi Order training and retreat format. Rather than six stages, Stein offers three that earmark the mid-life journey; 1) separation, 2) liminality, and 3) reintegration. These stages create a framework in which to understand the cracking of the persona, the search for the Self and the formation of an expanded identity which arises out of this process.

Stage I — Separation

Then a 'crack' can open in the identity between the ego and this persona, between 'who I now feel I am' and 'who I have appeared to be in my own eyes and in the eyes of others in the past.' The glimpse into this discrepancy can be terrifying. When that former identity and the dreams it was based upon get deflated and lost, there is a sudden realization of the ego's vulnerability and of the shadow personality, as well as of the limits on life's ascendance and on its expansive movements forward. (Stein, 1983, p. 7)

The central task of the first stage is to recognize the passing of an identity built upon the ego's association with the persona and its emphasis on the external. The deep anxiety experienced during this period is due to this separation from one's previous identity. With the mourning for this lost identity and its subsequent burial one may eventually give birth to the emerging Self.

The discovery of the Self and the gradual stabilization of its felt presence and guidance within conscious life, becomes the foundation for a new experience of identity and integrity, based upon an internal center, the Self, rather than rooted in externals, the cues and reinforcements from parental figures and other models, from cultural influences and expectations, and from collective pressures. (Stein, 1983, p. 27)

The period of separation in mid-life as articulated by Stein parallels Pir Vilayat's description of Stages I and II in his interpretation of the alchemical process. Here Pir speaks of disidentifying from one's self image and identifying with one's eternal archetype. During these stages, meditation practices are suggested for the purpose of discerning the essential elements of one's being, the divine qualities of the soul or Transpersonal Self, as opposed to the conditioning and transitory nature of the personality. The fuller recognition of one's own mortality is a catalyst in both men's teachings for igniting a process in which one reviews one's life and being in search of that which is of lasting eternal value.

Stage II — Liminality

Stage II is the full experience of the world of betwixt and between in which one's old self image has been buried but the new and richer sense of self has not manifested yet. Although periods of liminality appear throughout life, the mid-life period is usually its most powerful and extended time. Stein speaks of liminality as the threshold between the conscious and the unconscious.

> Liminality, Hermes' home, occurs: when the ego is separated from a fixed sense of who it is and has been, of where it comes from and its history, of where it is going and its future; when the ego floats through ambiguous spaces in a sense of unbounded time, through a territory of unclear boundaries and uncertain edges; when it is disidentified from the inner images that have formerly sustained it and given it a sense of purpose. Then the unconscious is disturbed in its archetypal layers, and the Self is constellated to send messages: big dreams, vivid and powerful intuitions, fantasies, and synchronistic and symbolic events. The function of these messages is to lead the ego forward, and this guidance helps it to do what it has to do, whether this is to enter liminality further, or later, to emerge out of it. (Stein, 1983, p. 22)

Stein further describes liminality as a time when the boundaries of the I and not I come closer together than in periods of fixed identity. Psychologically speaking, a person experiences this state as a time of being on the road, adrift or floating, for the I is homeless. The critical questioning of the nature of the I will eventually lead to the following breakthrough.

> It is within this descent into the dregs of liminal existence that there occurs an opportunity for consulting the Self that is not possible elsewhere. Here the self does not have the puffed-

up face of unlimited potential, as it may have had in former years. In this consultation with the Self, now an image of long-lived wisdom and foundational truth, clues begin to appear for what will become a person's sense of core and for the life tasks that remain to be carried out. (Stein, 1983, p. 109)

Pir Vilayat describes stage three in his six phase alchemical process as a complete dissolving of the identification with the personality; however, he stresses a direction not emphasized in Stein's work, which is the discovery of oneself as a transpersonal source of consciousness, emotion and life force or spirit. Murray Stein's treatment of the mid-life passage has been so meaningful to me because he has vividly articulated the pain, frustration, confusion, suffering, and stress I have experienced during this passage into liminality. I recognize my psychological trauma as the loss of my self image. Pir Vilayat accents one's capacity to ascend to the transpersonal dimension during this crisis period and forge an identity with the impersonal aspects. Practices given during this stage in the retreat process facilitate a loss of the individual self and a merging with the ground of being or unity consciousness. Pir Vilayat's approach offers the gift of union with the Spirit, provided it is not used to avoid psychological pain, as mentioned previously in John Welwood's writings on the spiritual bypass. During periods of liminality, when the personal sense of self has dissolved, there is the need to honor the psychological pain of this passage and the opportunity to experience a heightened awareness of the Transpersonal.

Stage III — Re-integration

The period of reintegration in Stein's treatment of mid-life parallels stages IV, V, and VI in Pir Vilayat's understanding of the alchemical process. Both are concerned with the building of a new identity which is more inclusive of the Self. The Sufi Order training and retreat format encourages restructuring of the personality to include a greater manifestation of the divine archetypes and qualities latent in the soul while Murray Stein writes of placing the ego in service of the Self. At this phase, both speak of the necessity of incorporating the polarities. For Pir Vilayat, it is the incorporation of what may appear as opposite qualities to the ego, such as truth and compassion. In **In Midlife**, this issue is addressed in relation to integration in the following manner.

The ego's tendency, however, is to solve the problem of opposites and the psychic tension they create by accepting one side (and identifying with it) and rejecting the other (and repressing it). (Stein, 1983, p. 138)

The ego's main search is for comfort, security and it seeks to avoid tension by one-sided identification, while the Self on the other hand is "made up of opposites and desires their 'marriage'." (Stein, 1983, p. 138)

The reintegration phase of mid-life is successful when there is "the conscious presence of the Self within the everyday world of ego existence." (Stein, 1983, p. 139) The same approach is found in the final stage of the alchemical process advocated by the Sufi Order, in which the initiate is encouraged "to maintain the supreme perspective while involved in life." Both Murray Stein and Pir Vilayat warn that this new reintegration must not lead to a fixed and rigid identity but must allow for future periods of liminality or disidentification which eventually leads to greater growth.

Hermes and the Spiritual Guide

Drawing upon his Jungian background, Stein believes the journey through liminality during mid-life is aided by Hermes, the God of transitions and the archetype of the unconscious. This archetype acts in the role of guide, messenger, protector and companion. In the Sufi Order training the spiritual guide functions in these four roles for the student and retreatant, thereby giving expression to the Hermes archetype.

In his role of guide, Hermes is the unconscious aiding the ego in coming to terms with deep transformational change. As the illegitimate son of Zeus, he represents the dimension which is outside of the collective assumptions and opinions of society. This enables Hermes to offer the traveler through mid-life a greater perspective upon the limitations of group or tribal consciousness and the persona. This is reminiscent of the process of unlearning in one's discipleship, previously discussed in Chapter III, in which the spiritual guide provides the student with alternative perspectives beyond the conditioning associated with the personality.

Hermes' primary function in mythology is to connect the gods and humanity through communication. According to Stein, Hermes is "the messenger sending function of the unconscious in the period of transition at mid-life and liminality." (Stein, 1983, p. 14) In the Sufi Order training the spiritual guide serves as the messenger communicating the dimensions, intentions, and movements within one's eternal archetype or Transpersonal Self to the student until the initiate realizes that Hermes aspect of him/herself.

Hermes' protection represents that part of us during mid-life which holds "a healthy suspiciousness of the intentions of alluring persons as illustrated by Circe in **The Iliad**." (Stein, 1983, p. 95) In the scene from Hazrat Inayat Khan's play examined in Chapter III, there were several examples in which students were seduced by the phenomenon of seeing fantastic auras or were caught in an alluring experience with a medium and the sage responded with just the right note of healthy suspicion which broke the atmosphere of infatuation. Functioning as a spiritual guide means occasionally giving expression to the Hermes role as protector, but without creating dependency or impinging upon a person's freedom to make their own decisions.

The wish for Hermes' companionship has two strands, one is the wish for journeying itself, for being on the journey and the other is a wish for intense intimacy and communion. (Stein, 1983, p. 131)

As mentioned earlier, Pir Vilayat's favorite metaphor for the relationship between the spiritual guide and student is that of a mountain climbing guide assisting a climber through the terrain of the mystical landscape. Both are continuously on the journey or the path and are bonded by the special intimacy and communion which shapes their unique relationship. One of the greatest gifts I have received from my service as a spiritual guide is the invitation into the deepest intimacy with people and the communion of hearts and souls that arises out of such a coming together. In the quest for radical naked intimacy, words used by Stein to describe the Hermes type of companionship, people have consistently shared with me, in my role as spiritual guide, secrets they have never told to anyone else. My response is to attempt to be fully present for and with them and in so doing share the intimacy of my own being.

In this section, the alchemical process of transformation was explored as developed by Pir Vilayat in the teachings, training and retreat format of the Sufi Order. The second half was focused upon parallels between the Sufi Order's approach to this theme and Murray Stein's treatment of it in the transition time of mid-life. The intention of the alchemical process as applied in the training of Sufi Order and a Jungian approach to a life passage can be mutually enriching for those seeking to integrate psychological and spiritual growth in a search for wholeness.

Bibliography

Bolen, J.S. **Goddesses in Everywoman**, New York: Harper & Row, 1984.

Jacobi, J. **Complex Archetype Symbols**, Princeton: Princeton University Press, 1974.

Jung, C.G. **Two Essays in Analytical Psychology**, New York: Meridian Books, 1956.

Khan, H.I. **The Complete Sayings of Hazrat Inayat Khan**, New York: Sufi Order Publication, 1978.

Khan, H.I. **The Path**, New York: The Sufi Order, 1985.

Khan, P.V. **Toward the One**, New York: Harper & Row, 1978.

O'Kane, A. "An Interview with Zalman Schacter," **Mureed's Newsletter**, 1985.

O'Kane, A. "Psychological Dimensions of Spiritual Counseling: An Interview with Elaine Resnick," **Mureed's Newsletter**, Spring, 1985.

O'Kane, A. "The Search for Wholeness: An Interview with Frances Vaughan," **The Heart and Wings Journal**, May/June, 1987.

Stein, Murray. **In Middle**, Dallas, Texas: Spring Publications, 1983.

Walsh, R. and Vaughan, F., (eds.) **Beyond Ego**, Los Angeles: J.P. Tarcher, Inc., 1980.

Welch, J. **Spiritual Pilgrims**, New York: Paulist Press, 1982.

Atum O'Kane, Ph.D., is a psychologist and is the Secretary General of the Sufi Order. This article is an edited version of a selection from his dissertation.

Some Parallels Between Sufi Practices And The Path of Individuation

By Mohammed Shaalan

Personal Background

In Egypt, medical education is modeled on the old British system; so that behavioural or psychosocial aspects of illness are not given much prominence in the understanding or treatment of disease. Psychiatry is mostly bio-medical. If there is any reference to psychotherapy, various schools are covered, with the psycho-analytic tilted Freud-wise. The lay analysts left in Egypt are few, and Freudian. To seek Jung was a deviation from the norm, almost an underground activity. Yet with the many parallels between Jungian psychology and prevalent Sufi practices in Egypt, it is surprising that Jungian psychology is not the prevalent approach.

My own personal development could provide a parallel. With my childhood years spent in a small village almost totally isolated from city life, and hence Western culture, my basic attitudes and beliefs were formed. Islam permeated the local culture at many levels: beliefs, values, religious practices, ethics, traditions and more. The Sufi groups or Tariquas (meaning 'ways') provided (mainly) the rural population with reference groups which had many functions, including the political one of belonging to an apolitical political group. A sort of informal network where people could seek refuge from overt political life. Yes, indeed it was such networking that enabled Egyptians to resist, passively yet persistently, many a cultural, political or even military form of invasion.

This subculture provides functions which, in a nutshell, could be described as paralleling the Jungian individuation process, which will be the subject of this chapter. In terms of ends and means, it provides a way or path in pursuit of a higher goal that is beyond the satisfaction of personal needs; a meaning and purpose in life that goes beyond individual life. The means depend to a great extent on the relationship between teacher (Sheikh) and seeker or pupil (Murid) mostly within a group context. Practices include spiritual excercises of a meditative nature (including the moving meditative practice of "Dhikr" and Dervish whirling) as well as selfless work expecially of a charitable nature. At the level of beliefs, teaching by symbol and allusion (such as through the use of parables, proverbs and examples) is geared towards the intuitive mode. Life stages and phases of psychic development are taken into account in guiding a seeker on the path. The ultimate pursuit is the attainment of a state of "Fanaa" or dissolution in unity with the Divine. It is a state of wholeness where the self, in its limited and transient nature, is transcended; and this often appears as a state of wholeness where dualities and contradictions are encompassed around a central self; in other words a process of individuation. Again, here the concept is different from individualism, for it entails belonging to a group, ascending through its stages to achieve the boundless and infinite nature of the Divine. On another dimension it includes the pursuit of wholeness or health at the physical level as well, where the healthy body is viewed as the manifestation of a healthy soul. Thus it serves the function of therapy for the person-as-a-whole.

From the subcultural background, its antithesis was provided by a British boarding school (Victoria College, Alexandria), then a medical university education (Cairo University), then several years' experience in psychiatry between Cairo University, England and the U.S.A. (Michigan). The recently acquired culture submerged the more deeply ingrained subculture. Yet with the maturation of years, the unfulfilled function wells to the surface. An alliance is made between the once submerged fringe subculture of the Orient and the subcultural fringe of the Occident. By the late sixties, Jung was being rediscovered by the lay person and the youth rebels. At Esalen (Big Sur, California) I too rediscovered Jung, or rather uncovered my original subculture, which paralleled so much of Jung's teachings; and, conversely, I rediscovered the wisdom in my childhood Islamic rural subculture through those teachings.

Thus even my knowledge of Jung was, like his teachings, more intuitive and immediate than systematic and intellectual. Expanding in the same ripple fashion, inner psychological knowledge spread to cover the outer. The individual was connected to the whole; society in its music and art to social and political activism, were all encompassed. Such was the path tread by Sufis and such the road to individuation.

However, the thinking function needed redress. Returning from a temporary migration to the U.S.A. I took a post as chairman of the department of Neurology & Psychiatry at Al-Azhar University which was just being established. It was an opportunity to sidetrack from the consensus of psychiatric education and research. The first doctoral thesis to be granted by the department was on the relation between psychotherapy and Islamic (Sufi) spiritual meditative excercises (prepared by Moustafa Abu-Auf, M.D., 1975-81). Jung was required reading.

With increasing involvement simultaneously in private psychotherapeutic practice in addition to interest in public issues, the thinking and the intuitive, coupled with the sensation and feeling, were welded in the heat of grappling with the immediate and living problems.

Merged in a growing Islamization of Egyptian culture and supported by a Western educational background, with a renewed interest around its fringes in the Orient, I saw myself as part of a bridging process between opposites, both inner and outer. I was living (rather than learning about) both Jung and Sufism.

For this reason the presentation to be outlined will follow the path of experience and practice rather than theoretical knowledge. Selected themes that are common to both Jungian psychology and Sufism will be presented with a view to demonstrating the parallelism.

Introduction

Sufism is the Islamic form for what is essentially a universal mystical essence of all religions. The mystical experience is an overwhelming event. Its subject cannot come out unscathed. It entails a transient sense of loss of boundaries that nevertheless seems eternal. There is a feeling of merging of what was once a self into that which was non-self. That non-self is experienced with numen, with a sacred quality that is non-describable, effete and joyful — a larger infinite Self.

Yet for many, that merger may be experienced as a dissolution, a loss, a symbolic death of the smaller self that was. That by itself, without the joy of rebirth into the greater Self and a communion with it, can be an overwhelmingly frightening experience, yet it is unforgettable.

For those who remember, life goes on and in a broader scope. Needs become less pressing while meta-needs become the main source of fulfillment. The self is accepted as it is, with its paradoxes and opposites. God created the self with its wrong and right.[1] There is the self that orders evil;[2] the self that reproaches;[3] and the secure (rested) self[4] that integrates them both as it transcends them, akin to the Jungian concept of integrating opposites in the process of individuation. In the end there is only one self: the self from which God created man and his (her) spouse.[5] There is no sexual specification as to precedence. Man here refers to humankind rather than man the male; and Adam is generally used in the same context. There is no precedence or preference between male and female. That too resembles another Jungian concept, that of anima and animus being integrated as an expression of individuation.

There are still higher states of consciousness that Islamic Sufis derive from the Quran. There is the self that is fulfilled (accepted by), well-pleased and fulfilling for accepting of (well-pleasing unto) God.[6] Further still is the self that is inspired or enlightened (Quran, Sura XCI, 7,8, ibid). For Jung also, individuation is not a final act but an endless process. The unconsious is likened to a bottomless ocean that is welling with endless images and archetypal memories.

Sufis are those who travel that path ceaselessly. An overwhelming event becomes a powerful on-going process. Very few can continue to tread that path. The rest either wallow in suffering or escape into the security of a highly structured life under the guidance of an overpowering leader. Some Sufis assume that role, and in doing so lose their freedom to proceed on the path of endless search. In order to offer

---

[1] Quran, Sura XCI. Al. Shams or the sun 7,8. "By the Soul, and the proportion and order given to it" "And its enlightenment as to its wrong and its right."

[2] Quran, Sura XII, Youssof, 53. "Nor do I absolve my own self (of blame): The (human) soul is certainly prone to evil..."

[3] Quran, Sura XLLLV, Qiyama or the Resurrection, 2. "And I do call to witness the self-reproaching spirit..."

[4] Quran, Sura LXXXIX, Al-Fajr or The Break of Day, 27. "To the righeous soul will be said O (thou) soul in complte rest and satisfaction..."

[5] Quran, Sura IV, Al-Nisaa, or Women, 1. "O mankind! Reverence Your Guardian Lord Who created You from a single Self created of like nature its mate,..."

[6] Quran, Sura LXXXIX, Al-Fajr or The Break of Day, 28. "Come back thou to thy Lord, well-pleased (thyself) and well-pleasing unto Him!"

a settled security to their herd they have to settle themselves. They join in adopting what their herd assumes are unshakable givens. They prescribe rituals, yet permit themselves to break them. A Sufi may commit acts which, for his followers, committing them could appear as sinning. For traditionalists (Sunnis) such paradoxical living is unacceptable. So is the case for most Sufis who regard such extravagances as eccentric.

Jung described the transformation of Goethe's Faust as he lived through his hidden and unacceptable self. Of those eccentrics, most prefer to hide their sins. For, aware of the modeling role for their herd, they only disclose that which is regarded by traditional belief as good. (Islam is often regarded as a culture of shame rather than guilt.) Yet it serves the purpose of preserving the paradoxical nature of being, combining good and evil, while providing the external binding social structure of the clear-cut dominance of good. Nevertheless some eccentrics cannot withhold their secret. They act good and evil, and express their Divine nature in human terms. Paradoxically they see the futility and danger of such disclosure, so they invite martyrdom. Al-Hallaj is the most notable example.

Here comes the grey area between the joy of mysticism and the agony of isolation, persecution, madness and suicide. Many are called, few are chosen. For the many, the overwhelming experience is a bad trip which one must both escape and cannot forget. There are those that cannot forget though attempting to. Boundlessness turns into exaggerated boundaries. Active self-transformation settles into rigid self-structuring. Psychosis gives way to character defects and fossilizing with chronic, rigid mechanisms of projection and introjection among others, such as paranoia and depression, as well as acting-out and internalizing psychic conflicts in restricted or encapsulated forms.

The persona becomes a rigid mask that serves to hide and bury the deeper self. The louder the call, the more rigidity in repressing it.

Such suffering souls rush to the leader who provides them with the needed structure. Himself a Sufi, he has chosen to voluntarily give up his freedom to metamorphose, in order to provide security for his herd and, inadvertently, for himself. In this sense he becomes an amputated Sufi. Such is the group illness that is contained when given that structure. The suffering is alleviated when shared with a group cared for by a leader. The more frightening the freedom, the more submissive the individual and the group, and the more dominant the leader. Such groups share suffering and seek relief in submission to such rigid structures. The leader acts out and vicariously fulfills their needs. In one such group a member was refused permission to marry an outsider of her choice. Her brother, recently arrived from completing his education, clashed with the Sheikh and physically assaulted him. In the police investigation the Sheikh's holiness and his psychic powers crumbled. There was no intervention from the Heavens as expected. The group subsequently crumbled. With the passage of time, its dispersed members, now forlorn and without a leader, though freed, did miss the comfort and security of their unfree days. Intellectually they perceive the imposture; but emotionally they yearn for it.

Meaning and Purpose

A highly qualified professional had been offered a handsomely paid job in one of the oil-rich neighbouring Arab countries. He suddenly decided to reject it along with all worldly matters in order to find recluse for meditation and worship in a mosque. There he spent several weeks and was sought by hundreds of companions and seekers. When a psychiatrist was asked to see him, he convincingly replied that certain decisions in life could not be judged by rational analysis; nor should they be. He gave examples from Islamic history of events where faith, generating intuitive judgement, (figuratively) moved mountains. He had intuitively arrived at the decision to relinquish worldly pursuits in favour of spiritual ones. He had found meaning and purpose in life which provided him with a serenity and inner satisfaction that no worldly success could.

The psychiatrist was a graduate of Al-Azhar. So he neither recommended commitment nor prescribed medication; but suggested that he be left alone until the acuteness of the experience (psychotic or mystical) subside; and so it did.

This is a commonly recurring theme — the midlife crisis. It represents the turning point in the development of Jung's thinking. Beyond satisfaction of the basic drives, which Freud ascribed to sex, and Adler to power, man would search for meaning and purpose in his life; in other words seek what has traditionally been offered by religion.

For many this turning point may be a transformation experience which could take a person on to a Sufi path. If, having gone through a similar attempt in adolescence, he has acquired a backlog of experience, he may be better equipped to take on the role of teacher. In most cases the role of seeker would be satisfactory.

The important factor that prevents this discovery of meaning from becoming a sheer delusion that isolates its owner in a paranoid state is that it is shared, both in the historical dimension within the long history of Sufi tradition and the geographical dimension within the many Sufi groups that are spread all over the country. Sometimes he may form his own group and lead. Sometimes he would join and follow or share, depending on the degree of hierarchy in the structure of the group. Rarely he may be alone. Occasionally he may be a teacher or member of a Sufi group without necessarily calling it so.

There are an estimated three million members of Sufi groups in Egypt. On the other hand, psychiatrists have not increased much beyond the two or three hundred figure which was there three decades ago (the explanation is that the oil-rich Arab states quickly absorb them as they cannot find a foreign replacement for Arab-speaking psychiatrists as they might in the case of other medical specialties). Many mental crises, whether we choose to include them in psychiatric diagnostic categories or regard them as peak experiences in the path of Sufism, go to Sufi groups. There they seek salvation. Some sheikhs are astutue enough to differentiate between the frankly psychotic and the potential mystic; they either refer them to a psychiatrist or handle them in their own ways.

The public, on the other hand, often does not differentiate; it may tolerate much psychotic behaviour as being due to spiritual forces, sometimes Satanic but at other times Divine: "Majthoub", meaning being pulled towards the Divine, and "Majnoun" meaning being insane, are similar in sound, meaning and appearance. Perhaps this tolerance for abnormal mental states on the part of society in general creates a lesser need for psychiatric institutions, indeed may provide a socially supportive system that prevents deterioration and outright psychosis.

The therapeutic factor in all cases is the search for meaning and purpose. It is a factor that once grasped can be used to guide therapy in all stages of life and not just the mid-life crisis; particularly adolescence, which often coincides with the parents' mid-life crisis. In the family therapy format both sides may help each other.

At the socio-political level this has its reflections. By middle age most parents would have either temporarily migrated to oil-rich Arab countries, or at least been enterprising enough to benefit from the money brought in by those who have migrated. Having satisfied their basic needs as well as their adolescent children's, they attempt to resolve the ensuing crisis by turning to religion; more often it is a pseudo-religion where rituals, rites, and appearances are adhered to without real questioning of their essential or innate value. Their adolescent children either follow suit, sometimes overdoing their reaction by becoming more extreme or, more often, turn the other way. In the latter case they would seek pleasure and intellectual complacency, turning towards drugs, sex or blind imitation of what they perceive as Western libertinism. It is the rest of the youth who show the extremes more flagrantly. In the face of the gross discrepancy in wealth between them and the rich they turn to religious extremism which may turn political revolutionary or, alternatively, to another form of pleasure-seeking as in crime such as stealing, rape, violence and drug peddling as well as abuse.

This has become a social problem because at that level social and political life has been bereft of meaning. Once, national independence seemed like a religious substitute, along with the dream of catching up with Western liberalism. At another time, it was Arab nationalism coupled with socialism which promised strength in the face of the major Western powers. Justice internally was another religious substitute. Marxism and other "isms" played an ancillary supporting or opposing role. After the 1967 debacle (the defeat in war with Israel), these religious substitutes failed to provide the same sense of meaning. Hence the quick turn to archaic religion which, because of its compensatory nature, lacked depth and acted as another form of pseudo-religion. More people turned to fanatic, politicized religious groups (Al-Jama'at al Islamiya), but many remained within the buffering structure of the traditional Sufi groupings. In this sense the Sufi movements were apolitical, in that they had no direct involvement in politics. But they were political in their very apoliticism, by protecting against both religious substitutes (nationalism, socialism, etc.) as well as pseudo-religion or politicized religion. They provided a higher level of meaning that gave their members a conviction of the victory of meek righteousness that could withstand the power and strength of the other religious substitutes, including pseudo-religion.

For the Sufi, outward behaviour, rites and rituals, were not essential. They were preoccupied with inner belief. They were confident of their durability, and so could watch the birth and death of other movements without being challenged. Their awareness of meaning and purpose went beyond that which could be measured by temporal or temporary success.

Guide and Seeker

The guide or teacher in Sufism relates to a seeker or pupil. The parallel is the doctor or therapist and patient or client.

Jung's important contribution in this area lay in the emphasis he placed on the real relationship, rather than the role relationship between both parties. Psychotherapy is more like a mutual interaction where genuine change in the patient can only be achieved by some parallel change in the therapist, hopefully towards the better in both cases. A therapist cannot totally insulate himself behind a sterilized gown and deal with the patient as an object. The interaction is human and bipolar.

The Sufi teacher likewise is affected by his followers as well as affects them. The process may entail selection, where the qualities of both complement and attract each other, or resemble and parallel each other. This may entail a modification of both to achieve that relationship, whether based on complementary difference or supplementary resemblance.

There are followers who seek an idol and if they do not find one, mold the teacher as such. Their belief in the spiritual powers and the righteousness of their guide eventually affects him in the same direction so that he eventually turns into a protective and overpowering idol. Sometimes a wise leader may be aware that this is a role he has chosen in order to fulfill the dependency needs of his followers, and occasionally seeks liberation from that role. But often he becomes entrapped in it and actually consolidates his power and encourages still more dependency.

Others tolerate eccentricities in their teachers' behaviour, that by anyone else would be condemned as sinful. The parable of Moses and Al-Khidr, which was one of Jung's illustrations of his concepts, is a source of inspiration. But in some cases eccentricities practised by some teachers may be excessive. One Sufi was accepted by his community, including the top civil administration, when he took to appearing in public, even on the mosque pulpit, in complete nudity. Others would grant themselves liberties to perform what, to the seekers, is only an illusion of sin; but like Khidr's acts they are signs of a Divine wisdom and have a hidden meaning. A teacher may occasionally prohibit a romantic relationship between a man and his wife. All this would be accepted without questioning but with a conviction that there is some hidden wisdom which the seekers' limited minds cannot apprehend.

A Sufi teacher displays paradoxes both in his teachings and his behaviour. The classic tale of Mulla Nasruddin (known in Egypt as Goha) illustrates this. Arbitrating between two opposing parties, he told each that he was right. When a third party objected to the contradicition, he told him that he too was right. The untold assumption is that Goha was the ultimate right and all other differences were illusory and relative and so were all paradoxes. The other tale about Goha (Nasruddin) and his purchase of a donkey from the market also illustrates this. Goha alternated riding the donkey while his son walked, then reversing the situation, riding along with his son, then walking along with his son. In all cases he was ridiculed. In a moment of spontaneity, he simply decided to carry the donkey, helped by his son, and to proceed heedless of people's mockery.

The use of paradox is not explicitly described as a technique in Jungian therapy; but the basis for it is there. Recently it has been given a name and clarified as a technique. Paradoxes serve to bring out a person from the complacency of accepting either/or concepts so that a different and higher state of consciousness is attained immediately.

With a Sufi, the use of paradox is not restricted to technique but is a genuine expression of his state of consciousness. By example and action rather than by preaching and teaching, a Sufi conveys directly to the intuition of his follower the paradoxical nature of truth.

On the other hand, there are Sufi teachers who accept their role as leaders of a group that has molded them according to their needs. These include the security of a structured set of rules, rituals and practices that are required by the seeker. Their minimum is an adherence to the basic tenets of Islam, with ritual prayer, giving alms and adherence to certain ethics. These are the Sufis that are socially and officially accepted, even contained by the traditionalists (Sunnis) as well as the political administration. They are permitted a legal format with a Higher Council of Sufis and a supreme Sheikh (currently Dr. Abul Wafa'l Taftazani, formerly vice rector of Cairo University and professor of Islamic philosophy). Such "Sunni" Sufis have even been allowed to occupy the top official religious post, as the one time Grand Sheikh of Al-Azhar, the late Dr. Abdel Halim Mahmoud. However, in their official statements they would be cautious enough not to make any eccentric statements that could offend the majority of Sunnis occupying positions in the Al-Azhar structure. There are other Sufis in Al-Azhar but mostly not in the limelight.

Their arch opponents are the Wahhabis of Saudi Arabia who have a political interest in supporting the extreme right-wing Sunni position and almost condemn Sufis as quasi-heretics. This throws light on the progressive and revolutionary nature of Sufi movements. As mentioned, their apoliticism in itself is a political position that threatens any form of oppression that can hide behind Sunni Islam. For the extreme Sunnis, as the Wahhabis (who provide the ideology for Saudi rule), only outward conformity is needed. You may rebel very secretly and sin, perhaps less secretly; the important thing is not to be caught and not to display but to hide such weaknesses. Semblance is above essence. That is all that oligarchies need, especially when bereft of an inspiring belief system.

Finally, there are those Sufi teachers who do not announce themselves as such, but emphasize their similarity to the accepted norm. Some in turn may not even know they are Sufis.[7] But in essence they perform the same function. Another Sufi parable demonstrates this: A group of three scholars went on a long journey seeking a well-reputed Sufi teacher. They were accompanied on the long journey by three muleteers who spoke nothing throughout the journey. When they met the famous Sheikh, they were well received and shown to their sleeping quarters. As they were closing their eyes they saw their long sought for Sheikh going toward the muleteers and paying homage to them. Realizing their mistake about who was the real teacher they tried to apologize to the muleteers. These refused, insisting that they were simple muleteers who had nothing to do with those scholars' philosophizing.

The Jungian therapist is also very human. His first paradox is that he is a human being with frailties as well as the magical image which the patient projects onto him (whether God-like or Satanic). He may bring his patient into a paradoxical state of mind by acting both as a role (ranging from God to Satan), and as a real person with human qualities. Not only that, but he shares and is affected by his patient's conflicts which he ultimately accepts as paradoxes natural to the concept of truth. He is passive in that he follows his patient's direction but he is active in that he may define that direction even before his patient has defined it and guides him along its course, giving him the freedom of choice to conform as he was or to develop and risk discovering the unknown. The therapist has no qualms about being human and about sharing his humanness with his patient. For the ultimate aim of therapy is to transfer the patient from a role (patient) to a real (human) position. This explains how such a therapist-patient relationship evolves towards the mutuality of a human relationship.

---

[7] The author includes the late President Sadat in this category; this is based on the description, in his autobiography, of an experience of a mystical nature that occurred while he was in prison isolation, and is further supported by other evidence from his behaviour, private and public.

Jung was known, and sometimes unjustly criticized, for his human relationship with his patients. He interacted, he shared, he developed internally with every patient who touched his depths. This parallels the same eccentricities which Sufi teachers are often wrongly accused of by their blind opponents. The parable of Khidr and Moses is telling again. Do not judge by appearances. There may be goodness behind what appears as evil.

This may touch on the sensitive issue of the nature and extent of intimacy between patient and therapist. Despite aberrations and abuses, there remains a situation where occasionally the "weakness" of a therapist, his assumption of a real human relationship with a patient, may be a factor in therapy. This must be delineated from situations where a therapist uses a patient to satisfy his own personal needs. Jung knew that and practised it courageously. Yet imitators cannot be exempt when accused of abusing the doctor-patient relationship. Similarly with Sufis. Some take liberties which in the end convey a message while others may use them to satisfy their own personal needs and abuse their followers. While Jung was not a practising group psychotherapist, his contributions in the realm of the collective nature of the unconscious, his excursions into social and group phenomena, his analyses of history, religion and, to a lesser extent, politics, all gave social meaning to his psychology.

Sufis experience their peaks individually, often after prolonged periods of isolation and meditation. However, they return to the group and attempt to guide others, indeed society, to the path. They function in groups. Sometimes they are social and political activists. Al-Hallaj travelled far and wide and was more a threat to political oppressors than he was to the orthodox. Theologians, nevertheless, when they crucified him, used his pantheistic statements as the excuse. In recent Egyptian history, Sufi movements played an important role in resisting British occupation.

Group therapy and social psychology have much to gain from Jungian contributions and have much in common with Sufi practices.

Symbol and Allusion

Both Jung and Sufis use symbol and allusion as vehicles for transferring knowledge. In Sufism, artistic symbolism is usually limited to geometric forms. The mandala is a recurrent figure in most Islamic designs. Other forms are literary symbols: the use of stories, proverbs, aphorisms, etc.

In this section, the use of a particular Sufi story will be shown as an illustration of how it could help troubled souls by touching on deeper layers of the unconscious. A particular story will be selected, namely the one derived from the Quran (Sura XVIII, Al-Kahf or The Cave) about Moses and Al-Khidr. It happens to be a story which Jung used to illustrate the process of individuation.

It is about the encounter between Moses and a wise, knowledgeable God-inspired man. (He is assumed to be Al-Khidr, the Qutb or pole of Sufis.) Moses asked to learn from him; Al-Khidr was reluctant, warning Moses that he may not bear with him. He accepted on the condition that Moses ask him no questions. They proceeded and ran across a boat that belonged to some fishermen. Al-Khidr punctured the boat and sank it. Moses objected. Al-Khidr warned and reminded him of his pledge. He apologized and renewed the pledge but broke it again when Al-Khidr, visiting a family, killed their boy who happened to have been a delinquent. The warning and pledge were repeated only to be broken a third time when Al-Khidr, coming to a village of thieves, proceeded to help them rebuild a falling wall. So Al-Khidr announced the parting of ways with Moses. But before leaving, he would explain his behaviour.

The boat was at risk of being confiscated by the tax collectors of a tyrannical ruler. Sinking it helped its salvation so that the poor fishermen could repair and reuse it. As for the boy, he was delinquent and his parents were Godly people who deserved a better child. They would beget him after the death of their delinquent boy who would have been a scourge and a source of suffering for them. As for the wall, it contained treasures that belonged to the orphans who inhabited the house. Rebuilding the wall saved the treasures by concealing them from the thieves.

This is a story that has caught Jung's imagination. In religious terms, it affirms to Muslims that God's will is wise, regardless of appearances to the contrary. A Muslim, in particular a Sufi, does not question God's will. What He chooses is always better than what he chooses.

This story was useful in helping patients in therapy understand the nature of their unconscious and the importance of accepting paradoxes as a step to integrating opposites on the path to individuation. The moving impact of this story in those cases is worthy of examination.

The first was a European lady married to an Egyptian. After establishing themselves abroad they decided to take employment in Egypt. The husband came from a middle class Egyptian family. The wife was obviously living an isolated life. This was partly due to her depressive nature. There was a history of attempted and completed suicide in the family. The father was alcoholic and often battered his wife and children. The patient had learnt to defend herself by threatening, and occasionally expressing, counter-aggression. She had bouts of severe depression. They had finally decided to seek psychiatric help. However, just one day prior to making the appointment, the illness had attained its tragic maximum. She decided to commit suicide; but before taking her own life she would take her two little sons' lives (aged five and three). During a quiet morning she stared into her son's eyes and seemed to be reading in them an expression of a wish to experience death. She took a kitchen knife and stabbed her older son repeatedly; and then she calmly proceeded to the next child. Then she went to the bathtub where she lay submerged in the water and immersed two bare wires connected to an electrical plug. She merely fainted. She had left a suicidal note for her husband. Shocked beyond description, he took her to a hospital then transferred her to a psychiatric hospital.

When she recovered, she had no recollection of the events. She was given intensive anti-depressive treatment (ECT and drugs as well as intensive psychotherapy.)

As she improved, she began to recall the events, develop insight and experience the severity of her depression.

There seems to be no rational or conventional frame of mind that can accept infanticide or suicide as a choice. Yet it could be regarded as God's will. Nevertheless, even though it was also His ordinance that we not kill our children or ourselves, it is God's will that his creature disobey Him and that he simultaneously aspires to obey Him. Yes, both opposites were God's will.

She realized her responsibility and accepted her incurable guilt. Yet she accepted God's will that she live to carry that guilt, and expiate it before finally executing herself.

Her determination to execute herself was expressed in a moment when she was unobserved. She squeezed her very slim body between the rails of a guarded balcony and jumped from the fourth story, feet down (she was still reluctant to fully destroy herself). She suffered severe fractures in her foot and pelvis as well as a ruptured spleen; but she survived. Furthermore, her depression was relieved.

She recalled the Sufi story which impressed her. She accepted God's will that she live, and dedicated herself to expiating her sin. She accepted her divorce, and visualized an ascetic life where she would dedicate herself to caring for orphans. She had previously been a nurse who worked with critically ill and dying patients. She had many encounters with death. The theme of death was a preoccupation with her.

She left for her home country where she continued to be under psychiatric supervision. She was able to function and received much support and sympathy from her folk. She kept in correspondence with the author, referring frequently to the help she received from the Sufi story, and to her relief in atoning for her act.

Some years later, correspondence ceased. It turned out that she had finally fulfilled her fate and successfully committed suicide.

The second case is that of a young man who had sunk into cynicism to the point of nihilism, using existential and nihilistic philosophies to justify his position. (In particular, he was impressed by Pink Floyd's "The Wall".) He had failed to progress in his university education. He asked his parents to provide for his travel abroad where he would try for a new beginning; but their symbiotic relation kept this suggestion at the level of fantasy. His paranoid belief that he was one of the select elite, whose mission was to convey the meaninglessness of life, led him to plan for a romantic self-destruction. Pitying his loving parents' anticipated grief, he decided to kill them first, in addition to his sister. He shot his mother as she was saying her prayers. She asked, as she was dying "Why, my son?" He answered in self-composure: "It is all for the best." His father had gone to the neighbours', seeking help. As he returned, he, too, was shot to death. The sister remained in hiding at the neighbours'. Then he proceeded to complete his romantic drama. He took the car and drove speeding towards the north, heading for a rock on the shore of a Mediterranean resort where he had fond memories. However, he realized that he had "forgotten" to load his gun. In all naiveté, he proceeded to the nearest police court where he asked the officer to lend him his gun in order to commit suicide. He was arrested and jailed in Cairo pending trial. He was subjected to psychiatric examination and proclaimed insane. However, the prosecutor was doubtful about the verdict. The patient was very effective in concealing his psychosis. Even his treating psychiatrist, whose assistance was sought by the parents as a friend of the family, with the request of treating the patient under the guise of being a friend, was oblivious to the seriousness of his illness. Naturally the patient concealed his illness here too.

He revealed that he had carefully concealed his illness when, some two years later, he was being reexamined. He admitted that he was indeed ill with crowding of thought, alternating with thought block; in addition there were phenomena of thought insertion, thought broadcasting, delusional perception, depersonalization and auditory hallucinations. However, he did not have insight into the delusional nature of his thought content.

In jail he had met with an arrested member of one of the religious fanatic groups (Al-Jihad). He helped him accept his act on the basis that what was committed during his atheistic period, he was not accountable for during his Islamic period.

With the various options presented to him, (execution, not guilty by reason of insanity, innocent) he was constantly drawn to the paradox of innocence together with the wish to be executed (or killed). He fantasied joining the Afghan guerillas so that he could die as a Muslim martyr. This was only a reverse version of his previous delusional wish to be killed which seemed to override the suicidal wish. He had toyed with the idea of shooting at the presidential guard in order to be shot back at.

This time it was he again that resorted to the Sufi story of Moses and Al-Khidr. It was all God's design, and there was a wisdom to it. He did not kill his parents, he asserted constantly; he saved them. Yet he had this persistent need to be killed. True, he attempted to cut his wrists while in jail, but did not succeed.

The story remains incomplete, but its lesson is there. The unromantic part of it is that he continues to believe in his elitism and in the Divine inspiration behind his acts. The tragedy is that his depression and guilt gave way to a paranoid grandiosity that, nevertheless, was devoid of appreciable emotional inflation. His perceived destiny was to be killed as a martyr, rather than commit suicide, and in the process kill still more innocent human beings.

The third case is of a young man, heretofore a bright and successful student, who suffered from bi-polar affective disorder. The initial manic attack was coloured with a delusion of being the awaited Mahd, the Saviour, another distorted Sufi belief. He was in a state of religious ecstacy with a fervour for delivering mankind from its suffering. He was treated with anti-psychotic medication and ECT, then maintained with Lithium carbonate as well as other drugs tailored to the nature of the phase (manic or depressive) that he was going through. Most of the subsequent manic attacks were milder. However, a common thread remained. This was reenforced by Sufi teachings which he constantly sought. (One of the wiser teachers suggested that a certain territory of his mind remain under psychiatric care). He was not repeating, as much as initiating his own ideas about the nature of his experience. His ecstasy expressed a sense of unity that permitted him to fuse lovingly with his physical and human environment. He realised, during clearer moments, that his pathology lay in the attempt to disclose or to convince others who obviously were not sharing his experience. His confidante was his therapist who could support him so long as he did not disclose. For Sufis, disclosure of their ecstatic experiences of unity would disqualify them. "For those who know do not speak; and those who speak do not know." (A Taoist aphorism which is very much applicable in Sufism.)

Again, the Moses-Khidr story comes handy during the manic phase. There is no guilt. That which happens is that which God wills to happen. This is coming to terms with the mania (for there is where most of the sins are performed, as in this case, though all were minor).

Therapy aspires to demarcate between the experience of pantheistic fusion with God and the reality of separation, so long as the self exists in its body. There is a certain grief in breaking off the symbiotic fusion and accepting the reality of separation, while simultaneously accepting the need to return to the state of blissful fusion. Coming to terms with the grief saves both the depression and the mania.

There is no happy ending in any of the three cases, but varying degrees of tragedy or misfortune or discomfort in one or the other. However, there is some wisdom that could be applied in milder, less tragic situations.

In all cases, the psychotic dissolution of boundaries, the fluid access to the unconscious, the acknowledgement of one's good and evil (both inspired by God), were all a hope for individuation. Clinically, they were all psychotic. In terms of outcome, treatment was in essence a failure. But in terms of process, the lessons to be learned could be transferred to other similar experiences which could transform a potentially psychotic experience into a healing process, striving for individuation beyond the limited goal of relieving symptoms or minimizing suffering according to the classical medical model.

Losing the barrier that protects the self from disintegration or fusion with the non-self is a common basis in psychotic experiences. It is also a turning point where a psychotic experience could be diverted into a form of mystical experience. In all cases it is a sine qua non for coming to terms with that unbounded reserve of wisdom in the hidden depth of the collective unconscious.

The unconscious is least accessible with rational modes of thinking. Hence the immense value of attempting contact by means of allusion, allegory, symbolism and other modes of communication.

Let us take an example from the opposite side. It is a more comprehensive example that illustrates the mutuality of patient and therapist in their quest for individuation, or Sufi liberation: social relation disguising a hidden agenda of a search for therapeutic assistance. In Islamic cultures, dispensing wisdom is a charitable act, one of the five corners of Islam (Zakat, giving alms, or charity). So, in a sense, doing psychotherapy for payment is un-Islamic.

However, if we take the (Jungian) therapist in T.S. Eliot's "The Cocktail Party" as charging only the liars and the fakes, his encounter with Celia Copplestone (from whom he received no payment) would fit in with Sufi "therapy" given within a social context, without charge, as a form of charity.

This is a case which one of my supervisees[8] in therapy was presenting and which happened, in its general form and indeed in some of its details, to resemble a case I had been seeing in my private clinical practice. So I shall present a mixture of his factual presentation and my hypothesization of its dynamics and meaning, based on the insights derived from that case as well as other experiences.

First the question of *casual therapy* within a non-professional relationship was brought up. It is not orthodox medical practice to give casual counsel or prescribe treatment without professionally conducted service, starting from role definition to payment of fees, maintaining a distance, taking a full history and conducting a proper examination, supplemented, if necessary, by ancillary investigations and finally prescribing treatment, not to mention keeping a file and issuing a receipt for tax purposes. Yet within the Egyptian cultural setting (and here again I am, especially in the realm of psychotherapy, referring to the influence of the Sufi tradition), the case is different. A policeman organizing traffic may keep the red light on pending receiving medical advice from the nearest doctor driver; a postman delivering mail to a physician may disclose a most intimate detail concerning his health condition; most amusing and frightening is the knowledge of the presence of a psychiatrist in a social gathering: he is either accused of analysing or seeing through the group or is asked to do so with the expectation that he not mention their weaknesses, in which case he would be safe but ignorant; or if he did, then would be resented, feared, challenged, opposed because of his having disclosed what was thought to be hidden behind the veil. To insist on ethical and professional

---

8 Muhammad Oweda, M.D. Staff, Department of Neuropsychiatry, Al-Azhar University.

standards in a categorical manner would, on the other hand, be regarded as snobbish or ungenerous. It was expected that doctors would radiate therapy as they moved about their daily activities, influencing any who as much as experienced their presence. After all, Sufis do that. They respond to any seeker for help and guidance, any time, anwhere. The more traditional Sheikhs insist on initiation into a group and total submission (like orthodox medical professionals). Yet people do recognize Sufis who are not surrounded by an organization of disciples or an aura of holiness. They recognize wisdom, even when disguised behind clowning or mockery or extreme modesty. Is not Goha (Nasruddin) still one of the sources of such casually distributed wisdom?

Such dispersion of wisdom, a form of counselling or psychotherapy, was expected of psychiatrists; especially if the psychiatrist (influenced by Jung) is aware of the power of religion and its nature as fulfilling a psychic function, regardless of how much knowledge he had in theology.

On the other hand, in our case the psychiatrist was aware of the factors in the personal unconscious which drove the patient to seek advice in a non-professional setting and only indirectly and in steps. There were dependency needs, seductive manipulations and testing, all of which he was able to see through as he decided to set the structure of his therapy session in this particular fashion. The general principle, however, was acceptable: that in our cultural setting, withholding wisdom was non-charitable, and radiating it, like a shining Mishkat or lantern moving quietly and unobtrusively among the crowd without burning or dazzling, was proper, especially from one who could be recognized (not officially but by the public) as a Sufi Sheikh.

Yet a Sufi Sheikh would be able, through silence, jest, or brief utterance, to give as much as the other party is willing to absorb. From those who are called and for the few who are chosen, each receives what is deserved. Only fewer still can tolerate to accompany the teacher throughout his journey. The greater the teacher, the fewer his followers, and the freer he is from being the shepherd of a herd. Al-Khidr had reluctantly accepted Moses for a follower, but even the great Prophet could not accompany him all the way.

Jungian therapists influenced by Sufism (or vice versa) wouldn't have a crowded clinic in Egypt. Yet they would have a large following outside their clinics; and some of their best clients could be often disguised as selected friends who are of a high spiritual and mental calibre. His charity is what he does with those masses who pick up glimpses as he moves among them and with those elites who distribute, in turn, to larger members whom they influence. For his professional practice, he is satisfied with a modest volume.

The case presented concerned a young, attractive lady, who recently put on a veil in pursuit of a religious form and structure that could obviate her inner need to attain individuation the arduous way. In other words, the "religion" she was seeking was a reaction-formation to the underlying conflict of opposites, a defense against direct experience of God; so she was opting for a solution for the paradox by seeing one side only (the religious) in the sense of obedience to norms and negating the other (the sinner) or one who acted spontaneously and with intuition. She had indeed sinned often, engaging in relationships with older men where she never really surrendered herself completely to fusing with them, whether emotionally or physically; but was always surprised when they finally decided to withdraw. The most painful one was when she was offered the role of mistress to a married man who categorically refused to marry her (polygamy is permitted in Islam), his excuse being that marriage would deromanticize their relationship.

The therapist, because of his own positive countertransference, insisted on seeing her in a public psychiatric facility (and therefore free of charge). After all, her final temptation was to attempt to seduce the therapist and, once succeeding, categorically regard men as "all like that", seductive and not satisfying (when in fact she had been doing just that, all the time, to men). In passing, she asked if a therapist finds out what she is suppressing, would he condemn and reject her?

The countertransference of the therapist, derived from his traditional rural background, would indeed condemn her. At the personal level, he regarded women as mothers fidelitous to their families, not enjoying sex as such, but reserving it for procreation. The patient knew intuitively that she had a basis for her doubts, even though on the surface the therapist appeared progressive and liberal. Indeed, unconsciously he rejected her; but his attraction continued as though he were working through his own schism. How could he accept women's equality, since he was indeed professionally and socially claiming to be progressive and liberal, when they were opposite in culture and temperament? He was, like her, unconsciously trying to resolve his inner conflict, and achieve individuation.

She was indeed helping him because her conflict was closer to the surface and pressing for resolution more than his. No wonder they divided their roles into therapist and patient. For therapy to be complete it had to induce change in both parties; but the therapist, being the carrier of responsibility, was the one who had to appear to take the lead. By "appear", I mean that in fact he was following the patient's natural healing towards individuation. He needed to help her see that she was not merely the sum of her sins, which were denied by reaction-formation. She had to take responsibility for her shadow and acknowledge it as part of herself, without splitting off or projecting it on to the Devil who swayed her from the straight path which she now chose. Putting on the veil and assuming religious manifest behaviour was her attempt to resolve the conflict by affirming her newly acquired persona while denying her unconscious shadow. The therapist was required to attain that himself simultaneously, if not in advance, at least at the level of vision and insight. Individuation, for a therapist of that make-up, means resolving his own dichotomies: poor versus rich, underdeveloped and oppressed nation versus imperialism, etc.; as well as his personal dichotomies: men versus women, madonnas versus prostitutes, mothers versus wives, etc.

Her path to individuation included stages: presenting the apparently "good persona", acknowledging, after an attempt to disown, her "bad shadow", and uniting them as one person, around a central self. The orthodox religious position would stop at denial and projection, by reinforcing the position of the apparently good persona and disowning the shadow. The persona would be the new-born, forgiven self — not the self that God gave us and enlightened it, so as to encompass its good and evil qualities.

Traditionalists accept the dichotomy and rely on a group or Sheikh who would reinforce their dichotomy and the projections. She was good, and the libertine woman and the men who joined her were bad; women (persons) who surrendered their will to the group and its Sheikh were safe in maintaining the dichotomy. For the therapist, he was good, and his political opponents were bad: the imperialists, the Zionists, the ruling capitalist class, even the ruling socialist bureaucracy; he was supported in his self-image by many a political group: the Nasserists, the leftists and to some extent the opposition, even the traditional politicized Islamicists in a sense. Neither internal nor external dialogue was accessible to his dualistic mind. Equal communication between opposing positions, internal balance between opposites, was a quality that both therapist and patient lacked and sought; but their mutual attraction was an expression of that need. With both being able to see both sides, both were a step away from individuation. She was intent on continuing the path; and he, at least, was flexible enough to risk changing. It was a mutual therapy (and, hence, in this way free of charge). Jokingly, colleagues in the group of supervisees assumed the charge would be in kind, mainly seduction as with his predecessors. But she chose him because she was after another barter: that she would complete her growth and individuation, if he, too, did. He had to be able to reevaluate her and resolve his ambivalence, which rejected traditional religion as reaction-formation, versus libertinism which his orthodox Islamic culture had conditioned him to condemn. He had to seek the path of direct knowledge of God, along with his patient. She was in that sense his companion and not merely a passive follower.

She had to see that she was her persona as well as her unconscious shadow, and she was both, rather than either, and in transcendence, touching on the collective unconscious, be, in addition, neither both nor not-both, but a personality encompassed around the central self which balanced all poles of the opposites.

This was the challenge of therapy. It was an uncommon choice for a search for individuation for both parties, also a choice to pursue the long and difficult Sufi path alone, without hiding in a group (Tariqua) and its leader (Sheikh).

Sufism and Jungian therapists have this in common. They are selective as to who is capable of pursuing the lonely path to its end, and who would fare better with a traditional therapist or join an Islamic group (Jamaa Islamia) or even join a Sufi group with similar structure to the traditional model (though not subject to its centralism). Many are called, few are chosen, and fewer still carry on the path alone to its end. The Sufi Guide and the Jungian therapist are both lonely wayfarers; but for that reason explorers of the unknown, treading its path without the security of a parental guide or outer fraternal structure. Perhaps their guide is the central self within, which coincides with the original self from which all were created, male and female, good and evil, divine and human.

Perhaps their company is in the knowledge that there are others travelling alone too, along the path. Both parties, Sheikh and seeker, therapist and patient, end up by this companionship: that their bodies, their personalities even, are separate and must part ways, yet maintain a union at the level of the universal self. They can become companions rather than friends who fulfill each others' needs or use each other in any way. Such is the combination between closeness and distance: we are one, yet we are two; and in that respect two whole people who do not complement or need each other in a personal sense.

(Although it could happen in the awareness of a network of such souls that communicate and support each other across personal or sensory boundaries: a sort of telepathic wavelength between such an enlightened elite.)

These were some case illustrations that may throw light on the deep journey into the unconscious and how it takes the risky path verging between the mystical and the psychotic.

Psychosis is an antithesis of mysticism. Though paralleling it, it may share a common root. For this reason, psychosis could, on occasion, be used as an opportunity for healing towards mysticism.

Sufis recognize this. They are also generally perceptive enough to make the distinction, leaving unto Caesar (psychiatry) that which belongs to Caesar; while taking on what they believe belongs to God, to their path in His pursuit. Yet the grey area is broad; and so many Sufi "Tariquas" (ways) do in fact perform a therapeutic function for mentally ill persons.

Psychiatrists in Egypt today are still in the lower hundreds; and most of them are restricted to the bio-medical approach. Even where psychodynamics are acknowledged, the Jungian view remains in the background. Their patients would not go far beyond the thousands.

On the other hand, Sufi groups have an estimated following of three million. Doubtless only few are chosen and successfully pursue the path. The rest are saved from collapse by the provision of a rigid structure with rites, rituals, guardianship and dependency, supporting the basic structure. Rather than florid psychoses, such followers would settle for obsessional, depressive, dependent and hysterical personality defenses; and some leaders' (teachers') paranoia or counter-dependency would comfortably fit in the symbiosis.

Conclusion

In conclusion, what has been presented here is no more than scattered themes that illustrate some parallelism between Sufism and Jungian therapeutic goals, particularly the road to individuation.

The truth is no clear-cut part of any dichotomy. The Truth is One and is found in Union. Words are too restricted to define it. Symbols — visual, auditory, motoric, even extrasensory and extramotor, or conceptually as allegorical, allusory, indirect intuitive, clairvoyant — are better instruments of communication than clear statements and rational interchange.

This boundless area is also frightening and ambiguous; it could even be maddening. Mystics and lunatics are different though they may share common qualities.

Teachers, guides, and therapists must be ready to travel with, and lead by following, subjecting themselves to the risks involved. Lone travellers pay their price in solitude, but real seekers will not let them migrate like Lao Tzu without leaving some Book of the Way, even if oral, indeed non-verbal. Sometimes those who know most say least; sometimes they act and at other times act better by non-action, their mere being acting as a source of radiance.

Their personal make-up, coupled with the rural Islamic culture which is mostly biased towards Sufi practices and insights, prepares therapists to understand and apply Jungian ideas and practices. This also fulfills the required recognition by Western culture and the professional community that one could be Jungian and not merely a Sheikh. Conceptually and in practice, there are many parallels and resemblances. What has been mentioned was for illustration and not meant to be comprehensive.

In both, religion in its different forms (outer and inner) serves a healing function, and there are different paths for different individuals. Each individual has his path. In common is the search for meaning and purpose, rather than interpretation as explanation.

The search is a plunge into the unknown and a choice from among the ambiguous.

There are lone seekers, and those who, having reached, lead by example, and others by leading with followership; but more often learning and discovering involves mutuality, involves interaction and mutual affection — the leader follows and the follower leads. The hands of God through the living unconscious guide.

There are so many themes that are equally illustrative, but the list was not meant to be comprehensive. For example, the issue of forming a school based on some sort of idol-worship is something that neither Jung nor the Sufis promoted. For the impact of Jung is not necessarily in his "Jungian" disciples or followers, if indeed there is any such body, but more on others from so many a field — history, mythology, art, sociology, anthropology, religion and more. Sufis, too, though they may have schools, have their deepest impact on many who do not even profess to be Sufis, even on many who are not Muslims or even religious in the traditional sense. In fact there are Sufi groups in Egypt that comprise Christians. Orthodoxy, doctrinairism or rigidity, are against the essense of the message in both cases.

On a more conceptual level one can further research the formulations regarding the nature of the psyche, the unconscious, the levels and nature of consciousness and its evolution. In both cases, one can find common elements that expound those concepts far beyond what more traditional schools of psychology have attained.

It is hoped that this presentation can act as a stimulus for interested scholars to venture into further details and depths; hopefully to find areas where the wisdom of Sufi tradition can be conceptualized in current psychological terms. If this is further coupled with the findings associated with recent research on bio-feedback as well as biological brain studies, we may be in for a new space age with regard to the scope of the human psyche, and the integration between physical laws and spiritual phenomena.

Mohammed Shaalan, M.D., is Professor and Chairman of the Department of Neuro-psychiatry, Al-Azhar University, Cairo.

Active Imagination In Ibn 'Arabi and C.G. Jung

By J. Marvin Spiegelman

C. G. Jung's remarkable autobiographical memoirs (Jung 1961) have made his ideas accessible to a large western public. The many who have read that book have been made aware of the tremendous importance that Jung attached to imagination as the organ of the soul, so to speak, and the *via regia* by which one can come to self-knowledge. Jung's discovery/invention of the technique of active imagination, a way of dialoguing with the unconscious, is dramatically described in that book in a way that the non-professional reader can appreciate and comprehend.

We are sympathetically drawn to Jung at 37, alone and adrift, separated from his mentor, Freud, and floundering about, knowing the importance of myth as a basis for the psyche, but believing that he had none. He tells us how he began to play with pebbles and sticks and water, building little villages just as he had done as a child, enacting what the unconscious itself suggested. Gradually, figures emerged in his play and he embarked upon a several-year journey entailing dialogue with those figures, leading him to practically all the ideas that he was to work out the rest of his life. Shadow, anima, wise old-man and woman, mana personality and self were all to reveal themselves in that imaginative activity. When he discovered that some of his patients came up with similar material when using that method and when he also found that many of his notions were already anticipated by alchemy, he felt safer in writing about it. He did not publish his initial paper on the technique of active imagination, however, until forty years later (Jung 1916/1957).

Although Jung's researches into alchemy made him aware of the many contributions to that art from the Arab world, he seems not to have known about the work of some outstanding Islamic mystics. This may not be so surprising, however, when one realizes that it was also only many years later that the work of mystics in Judaism became accessible to a larger public, largely through the efforts of Gershom

Scholem (1941). The mystics of Islam were almost equally unknown. Mystical experience itself was certainly paid attention to by Jung and his own dreams of this nature were reported in his memoirs. The powerful and ecumenical visionary experiences that he had in his seventies, combining Greek, Jewish and Christian symbolism, are particularly compelling. The rich heritage of Islamic mysticism, however, such as the writings of the astounding Sufi Master, Ibn 'Arabi, became available to a non-specialist public only in the late 1950's thanks to the splendid work of the noted French professor, Henry Corbin (Corbin 1958/1969).

That imagination played a central role in the thinking of both Jung and Ibn 'Arabi is readily apparent. Less apparent is the kind of relationship to imagination that each developed. Corbin even entitles his book *Creative Imagination in the Sufism of Ibn 'Arabi*, and uses the term Active Imagination interchangeably with it. Jung's understanding and use of active imagination, however, is somewhat different. (See "The Transcendent Function", 1916/1957.) In this paper, we shall summarize Corbin's presentation and compare the views of Ibn 'Arabi with those of C.G. Jung. It will be assumed that the reader is familiar with Jung's ideas to some extent, at least insofar as they are conveyed in his memoirs, and more attention will be paid to the perhaps lesser known conceptions of Ibn 'Arabi. Our aim is comparative.

At the outset, one can already say that it is quite remarkable that a lonely Swiss psychiatrist, open to his own psyche, should have experiences which are so similar to that of an Islamic mystic of the 12th and 13th century. Yet perhaps it is not so startling after all, since Jung believed that he was scientifically engaged and discovering structural properties of the psyche itself. That, unbeknownst to him, others in several different cultures and times had experiences similar to his can either confirm his efforts or enable the critic to further pejoratively characterize Jung as a "mystic." Here, however, we will attempt to continue the scientific effort by means of comparison and, one hopes, we will further understand imagination and the methods these hardy pioneers used in arriving at their convictions.

Unfortunately, space does not permit even a reporting of the experiences of either man. The interested reader can find them in the memoirs and in Corbin's book. We must, however, provide at least the flavor of the Sufi Master's writing, if only to illustrate the centrality of imagination in his work. The man who said, "He in whom the Active Imagination is not at work will never penetrate to the heart of the question," went on to describe how such efforts effected him (Corbin, 1969 Note 13, p. 382):

> This power of Active Imagination attains in me such a degree that it has visually represented to me my mystic Beloved in a corporeal, objective and extramental form, just as the Angel Gabriel appeared to the eyes of the Prophet. And at first I did not feel capable of looking toward that Form. It spoke to me. I listened and I understood. These apparitions left me in such a state, for whole days I could take no food. Every time I started toward the table, the apparition was standing at one end, looking at me and saying to me in a language that I heard with my ears, 'Will you eat while you are engaged in contemplating me?' And it was impossible for me to eat, but I felt no hunger; and I was so full of my vision that I sated myself and became drunk with contemplating it, so much so that this contemplation took the place of all food for me. My friends and relatives were astonished to see how well I looked, knowing my total abstinence, for the fact is that I remained for whole days without touching any food or feeling hunger or thirst. But that Form never ceased to be the object of my gaze, regardless of whether I was standing or seated, in movement or at rest.

Jung's experiences seemed to have been just as engrossing, if not so totally overwhelming. And this, too, we will be comparing later on. Here we will first present Ibn 'Arabi's approach to active imagination, followed by a selection of basic ideas which emerged from his work. Some connection with Jung's ideas will accompany this presentation, but a final section will be devoted to similarities and differences between them. (Page references, unless otherwise indicated, will be to Professor Corbin's basic volume).

Definitions and Methods

For Ibn 'Arabi, the function of imagination is theogony, a way of apprehending the divine. He says (p. 146):

> We can...take (God) as an object of our contemplations, not only in our innermost hearts but also before our very eyes and in our imagination, as though we saw Him, or better still, so that we really see Him.

God-centered imagination is active imagination and has several functions. One of these is to guide sense perception, focussing it so that mere sensory data is transmuted into symbols. This is the function of the *ta'wil,* as we shall see later on. The effect of this molding is to make perception, as well as imagination, theophanic. Corbin picturesquely states that "The Burning Bush is only a brushwood fire if it is merely perceived by the sensory organs. (p. 80)." For it to become theophanic or trans-sensory, active imagination is needed. This perception, like active imagination, takes place in a mid-zone, a region between Heaven and Earth, which is called *'alam al mithal.* This region seems to be equivalent to what Jung called "psychic reality."

A second function of active imagination is to place the opposites of spiritual and physical, invisible and visible, in sympathy. Indeed, the very degree to which the individual apprehends the divine is based on the degree of reality invested in the Image. The Image, however, is not outside of the person, but is "within his being, indeed is his very being, the form of the divine...which he himself brought with him in coming into being (Corbin, p. 156)."

The human capacity for imagination is parallel with the divine capacity. God possesses the power of imagination. By imagining the Universe, God created it. This idea — that the divine created the Universe from within Himself, via his imagination — is also known in esoteric Christianity, and is central in mystical Judaism. For Ibn 'Arabi, man's active imagination is also the organ of theophanic imagination; it "creates" God, just as God created human beings, but the image created is God revealing Himself to Himself.

> I was a hidden Treasure, I yearned to be known. That is why I produced creatures, in order to be known by them (p. 183).

Ibn 'Arabi follows the Prophet here in understanding that before there was visible creation, the Lord was "in a Cloud; there was no space either above or below (p. 185)." This Cloud, which the Divine Being exhaled and in which He originally was, receives all forms and gives beings their forms. It is unconditioned Imagination. The process of manifesting Himself to Himself is done via the divine's multiple Names, which is the particularization of all the unique qualities, including all the infinite variability of beings. This process of manifesting Himself to Himself via the "Names" (the particularities) is Active Imagination.

The conception of the original "Cloud" is strikingly similar to that found in Jewish mysticism and also in Jung's "Pleroma," in his *Septem Sermones ad Mortuos* (1925). It is a remarkably visual representation of the idea of the self as the original archetype, out of which are differentiated all the archetypes. Among the original conceptions of Ibn 'Arabi, is the idea that there was a divine sadness which resulted from the non-knowledge of His names. This sadness descended as divine Breath (*Tanaffus*) which is also Compassion (*Rahma*). The human being's longing or nostalgia for God is the same as God's longing for these separated parts of Himself. The parallels here with Jewish mysticism are remarkable, but space does not permit an examination of them. (See Scholem, 1941 and later works.)

The same power of Imagination, which is world-creating in God, exists in man as even God-creating (see below). This power of imagination (*quwwat al-khal*) makes possible our human potentialities for manifestation, inner or outer. Creation, in the sense of an unceasing theophanic imagination, is renewed from instant to instant. There is, therefore, a continuous succession of Being and beings. Imagination both creates and reveals this Hidden Being, but also veils it in other ways. The veil can be opaque altogether, which is the ground of idolatry. But it can become very transparent, depending upon the spiritual work and level of the person. Illusion occurs when the transparency is totally lost. This creation can appear in dreams or the waking state (p. 188). The function of the human being's active imagination is to create a bridge, to join two banks of a river, creator and creature. This is necessary for the continuous ascent of the soul, creating new theophanies.

The intermediate world of images produced by theophanic perception and active imagination call for a hermeneutics (*ta'wil*) or interpretation, because it carries a meaning which transcends the simple datum given and becomes symbol. This is similar to Jung's understanding of the symbol as expressing a depth or meaning which transcends all the particular "signs," conveying the content in the best possible way. Because active imagination creates new theophanies, there is the need for *ta'wil*. This seems to be a method of linking particular manifestations with ultimate forms. As Corbin expresses it (p. 209):

> Because there is Imagination, there is *ta'wil* ; because of *ta'wil* there is symbolism; and because there is symbolism, beings have two dimensions. Hence opposites, and all pairs require a union, *unio sympathetica*.

Another way of expressing this function of active imagination in unifying the opposites is given by a disciple of Ibn 'Arabi, Abd al-Karim Jili, who tells us (p. 214):

> Know that when the Active Imagination configures a form in thought, this configuration and this imagination are created.

But the Creator exists in every creation. This imagination and this figure exist in you, and you are the creator (*al Haqq*) in respect of their existence in you. The imaginative operation concerning God must be yours, but simultaneously God exists in it.

And Ibn 'Arabi himself says (p. 190):

Everything we call other than God, everything we call the universe, is related to the Divine Being as the shadow (or his reflection in the mirror) to the person. The world is God's shadow.

Ibn 'Arabi considers the method a "science of the imagination" (*'ilm al-khal*), and is both theogonic (in that the divine Names are realized in the work) and psychological. The theogonic aspect is found when one meditates on the Cloud. The primordial Cloud is intermediary between the divine essence (hidden) and the manifest world of multiple forms. The imaginal faculty relates to this intermediary, subtle region (*'alam al-mithal*) and thus produces theophanies. Dreams are between ordinary consciousness and the mystic state. There seems to be no recognition of the appearance of theophanies in dreams, unlike that found in Jung, in Greek religion and in Judaism also. But the theophanies of the various world religions, what Ibn 'Arabi calls the "God created in the faiths," are also to be found here. We will consider this "God created in the faiths" later on.

The psychological aspect of the "science of the imagination" is found in the distinction between two kinds of imagination. The first arises from the direct provocation by conscious processes and is called "conjoined" because these images belong to the subject personally, live and die with him. They may also arise spontaneously to consciousness, like dreams or daydreams, but they lack the "theogonic" quality. The second psychological aspect is found in those images which are independent and exist on the plane of the intermediary world. They are autonomous and continue functioning even when the person is not alive. Even these autonomous images govern the conjoined imagination. It would seem that Ibn 'Arabi is here giving distinction to what Jung would call the archetype *an sich*, or the primordial forms, as contrasted with the particular archetypal images which change from person to person, culture to culture, time to time. The theogonic forms can also be seen exteriorly, but only by mystics. Ibn 'Arabi says (p. 223):

Thanks to his representational faculty (*wahm*), every man creates in his Active Imagination things having existence only in this faculty. This is the general rule. But by his *himma* the gnostic creates something which exists outside the seat of this faculty.

This *himma* is a power of the "heart", a kind of eye by which God knows Himself, reveals Himself to Himself, experienced by the person in his active imagination. The word refers to meditation, conceiving, imagining. This "heart" is seen as a subtle organ, or subtle body, in which are found a number of psycho-spiritual organs, or centers. This view is remarkably like that described in great detail in Hindu religion (*chakras*) and in Kabbalistic Judaism (*Sephiroth*), as well.

The full functioning of this power makes it possible for the manifestations of the imagination to appear in the outside world. In other words, thanks to Active Imagination, the gnostic's heart projects what is reflected in him. For example, when the Angel Gabriel took the form of Dahya, an Arab youth known for his great beauty, the Prophet's companions saw only the youth, they did not see the Angel. Prayer (which we will discuss later) gives objective body to the intentions of the heart. This is also credited to Active Imagination, which gives what we would call psychic reality. The mystic is enjoined to "be as a Koran in one's own person", that is, to be so united with the Creator that no false discriminations take place. When one is "being a Koran", interestingly enough, the evils of dogmatism are overcome by transcending them.

The main function of Active Imagination is that of liberation. The process enables one to transform everything experienced into a symbol, finding the correspondence between the hidden and the visible. Jung's synchronicity seems to be a parallel. It is the *ta'wil*, a unification of the hidden and the manifest, which accomplishes renewal and creation. Many take this literally, rather than symbolically, and are destructive thereby.

Rather than the literalism generally found, Ibn 'Arabi recommends that one attempt to see the Lord with the inner eye. To accomplish this, one needs to develop a capacity for being in the presence of the divine with both vision and audition. If one does not see, he is then advised to worship Him as though he saw Him. Ibn 'Arabi says (p. 262):

> Let the faithful represent him by Active Imagination, face to face in his *Qibla* (prayer place), in the course of his intimate dialogue.

Ibn 'Arabi on God, Self, Prayer, Faith

Having examined what Ibn 'Arabi understands by active imagination, including several ideas which emerged from his meditations, we can now approach some of the main contents of the Sufi mystic's formulations. In general, we can ask, what are the events and processes perceived by active imagination? We have already recognized that for Ibn 'Arabi active imagination is theogonic creativity: in that kind of meditation one both perceives and "creates" God; the God created is a consequence of divine sympathy and compassion for men; He who receives Himself from Himself is to be found in that same human imagination.

But Ibn 'Arabi distinguishes between Allah, as God in general, and Rabb, or the particular Lord, personalized in an individual and undivided relation with His worshipper. He often says that the individual can not know God in His essence, since that transcendent Being is hidden and goes beyond all our individual and collective capacity. What we can know, however, is that individual Name which is vouchsafed for us in our very being. This sounds very much like the Self of Jung's psychology, the divine images as revealed in the individual's own psyche. Professor Corbin states, however, that this Self is neither impersonal nor psychological. He quotes the Sufi theosophical dictum (p. 95):

> He who knows himself knows his Lord. Knowing one's self, to know one's God; knowing one's Lord, to know one's self.

Corbin thinks that this is not the impersonal self, nor the God of dogmatic definitions who can subsist without any relation to the individual. Rather, it is the God who can know himself only "through the knowledge that I have of him, because it is the knowledge that he has of me." Yet this is precisely the understanding that Jung had of the Self in the psyche of the human being: mutual realization occurs through the relationship. That God needs man was the central realization of Jung's great opus *Answer to Job* (Jung 1952). Perhaps that work was not available to Corbin when he undertook his own magnum opus. In fairness, however, Jung also describes symbols of the Self, such as mandalas, which are more abstract and transcending our human condition. Yet the fact that even these are available only through the psyche itself was crucial for Jung, in his view that we can only apprehend the Self through this same human psyche.

Ibn 'Arabi expresses the view, that the self is the vehicle to God, in a number of impressive ways, one of which contrasts those who pray for compassion versus the mystics who ask that Divine compassion be fulfilled or come into being through them. He says, in his forthright manner (Note 26, p. 301):

> There is no point in asking God to give you something. That is the God you have created in your faith, He is you and you are He. You must fulfil (*tatahaqqaq*) yourself as much as you can through the attributes of divine perfection, among them Compassion. This does not mean that you will become God one fine day, for you are this God in reality, that is to say, one form among the forms of God, one of His theophanies. When Compassion (*sympatheia*) arises in you and through you, show it to others. You are at once Compassionate (*rahim*) and object of Compassion (*marhum*), and that is how your essential unity with God is achieved...When God sympathizes with one of His servants, this means He causes Compassion to exist in him, that is through him, so that he becomes capable of sympathizing with other creatures...God does not take him as an object of Compassion, but invests him with this divine attribute, whereby he experiences compassion for others.

In other words, when the worshipper is in direct connection with his Lord, he is being and expressing the divine Name that he was meant to fulfill. He becomes aware of his own "eternal individuality" (*'ayn thabita*) and knows himself as God knows him. This is certainly a very close parallel with how Jung understood the Self/ego axis in psychology. The similarity arises, no doubt, from similar experiences.

Ibn 'Arabi also finds a place for religious experience in a non-individual fashion. "God created in the faiths" is well-recognized and honored by him. He enjoins the seeker to embrace the divine Names in all faiths. He says (p. 119), "Let thy soul be as matter for all forms of all beliefs." That remarkable ecumenism is even placed at the highest level, for the one who can attain such a capacity is an initiate (*'arif*) or "One who through God sees God with the eye of God." This surprisingly complex paradox is based on the awareness that all beings carry the divine Names, and the divine Sadness, yearning to find a compassionate servant for all His Names, is the basis. Ibn 'Arabi even finds a place for the refusal of the divine Names, which for him includes not only atheism but fanaticism as well. Both of these arise from an ignorance of that same divine Sadness, but all will ultimately find their place with God, just as the believer will.

The totality of the universe, says Ibn 'Arabi, is made up of all the divine Names. Each being is an epiphany of his own Lord (*al-rabb al-khass*), which is to say that he manifests only that particular aspect of the divine Essence, that individualized Name. Furthermore, no determinate or individualized being can manifest the divine in its totality. "Each being has as his God only his particular Lord, he cannot possibly have the Whole (p. 121)." This outstanding insight of Ibn 'Arabi not only provides the reasonable humility which militates against dogmatism, it anticipates the highest kind of relativistic thinking available to us only in the latter half of the twentieth century.

All the individuations and personalizations of the divine, as realized in the unlimited number of Names, refer to the one and same Named One. The analogy used, as is so often the case with religious experience, is that of a glass receiving light. Each glass receives the light, but gives it its own coloration. Each of the infinity of Names or types of receiving vessels of glass carries an essential quality, each different from the rest, and each Name refers to "God who reveals Himself to and by the Theophanic Imagination (p. 192)." Corbin is particularly articulate here regarding the important paradox of the unity and plurality of the divine (elsewhere sometimes called the problem of "The One and The Many"). He says (p. 192):

> To confine oneself to the plurality of the Names is to be with the Divine Names and with the Names of the world. To confine oneself to the unity of the Named One is to be with the Divine Being in the aspect of His Self (*dhat*) independent of the world and the relationships...[both are necessary]...To reject the first is to forget that the Divine Being reveals Himself to us only in the configurations of the theophanic Imagination, which gives effective reality to those divine Names whose sadness yearned for concrete beings in whom to invest their activity...But to miss the second is to fail to perceive the unity in plurality. To occupy both simultaneously is to be equidistant from polytheism and monolithic, abstract and unilateral monotheism.

In this paradox, it is important to remember that God is only visible in his particularities and even the "God revealed in the faiths" is disclosed only partially. God is experienced only according to the "eye" that sees Him, and the faith reveals the measure of capacity. This is why there are many different faiths. For each believer, his faith is the true one; if God manifests in a different faith, the believer rejects Him and that is why they are in combat. To a true gnostic, all faiths are theophanic visions; only such a person, says Ibn 'Arabi, can have a true sense of the "science of religions." Finally, each of us can comprehend only his own Lord. The dogmatist is unaware of the metamorphoses of the divine and will be shocked that on the Day of Resurrection, even the unconverted rebel will receive Divine Compassion.

Creation, furthermore, is the rule of being, and this manifests at every instant. The Divine hides in one being, and manifests in another. It is a process of manifestation (*zuhur*) of the potential or hidden (*batin*). Corbin summarizes this process as follows:

> *Fana* (annihilation) symbolizes the passing away of forms that appear from instant to instant and their perpetuation (*baqa*) in the one substance that is pluralized.

People need to assist one another, says Ibn 'Arabi, to go beyond the faiths (p. 206) and advance spiritually. This ascending movement involves not only human beings, but all being. Individualizations ascend toward the divine and the latter descends into concrete individual existence. This formulation is exactly like that of Kabbalah, just as the statement that other worlds exist already in this world in every moment is similar to Zen. Each person's task is to know one's Angel or Lord, constituting an eternal pair. But people tend to confound their own Lord with the Divine Being as such, and then try to impose Him upon all. This kind of monotheism is the dark side of the "God created in the faiths" and produces hypertrophy and imperialism. This formulation of hypertrophy comes very close indeed to that formulated in Jewish mysticism, wherein it is understood as a manifestation of evil.

We come now to the role of prayer and its relation to active imagination. First of all, Ibn 'Arabi points out that prayer is not a request for something; it is an expression of a mode of being, a way of existing and causing to exist. Prayer is the highest form of Creative Imagination, in which the divine Compassion becomes theophany, is manifested. The "Prayer of God" is the desire of divinity to come forth from His unknownness and to be known; the "Prayer of man" accomplishes this via Active Imagination, and receives God according to his capacity. The dialogue that takes place is called *dhikr*, signifying "intimate dialogue," among other meanings.

Ibn 'Arabi sees prayer as taking place in three stages (p. 248): (1) One should place oneself in the company of his God and converse with Him; (2) Imagine (*takhayyul*) God as present, facing him; (3) Attain to intuitive vision (*shuhud*) or visualization (*ru'ya*), contemplating his God from his subtle heart center, simultaneously hearing the divine voice vibrating in all manifest things, so much so that he hears nothing else. Attaining this level of intensity, he recites the opening verses of the Koran.

We may now turn to a comparison of Ibn 'Arabi's approach to imagination with that of C.G. Jung.

Comparisons

Those who are familiar with the work of C.G. Jung will find a remarkable resemblance between his concept of the Self, of the divine principle found in the human being, with that formulated by Ibn 'Arabi. It is even more surprising that the collective images of the divine — as found in the traditional religions — is differentiated by both of them from that found in the soul of the individual. Corbin sees this clearly when he says (p. 266-267) that "It is psychologically true to say that 'the God created in the faiths' is the symbol of the Self. But the one who knows that the One God lies beyond can free himself from limited dogma." We might say that there is the Self of the collective religions and the Self of the individual, and it is the remarkable fate of Ibn 'Arabi and C.G. Jung to have discovered this difference, independently.

Corbin also reminds us that the Quran already has this possibility revealed in it, as shown in the verse (XXIV: 41): "Each being knows his prayer and his form of glorification." With this basis, Corbin thinks that the 'life of prayer' practiced according to Ibn 'Arabi "represents the authentic form of a 'process of individuation', releasing the spiritual person from collective norms and ready-made evidences and enabling him to live as a unique individual for and with his Unique God" (p. 268). Or, to quote Ibn 'Arabi once more (p. 271):

> God (*al-Haqq*) is your mirror, that is, the mirror in which you contemplate your self (*nafs*), and you, you are His mirror, that is the mirror in which He contemplates His divine Names.

The foregoing quotation is a remarkable presentation of this concept/experience and it is very much allied to the psychological concept formulated by the C.G. Jung who wrote *Answer to Job* (1952). Furthermore, when Ibn 'Arabi rejects the traditional mystical notion that a person can be "one with God," he also parallels Jung's ideas about ego and Self. Indeed, Ibn 'Arabi's conception of the God who is the "celestial pole" of one's being, is quite near to the Jungian concept of the "ego/Self axis." Both men are cognizant of the idea that consciousness always involves an "I and Thou," the total union of which results in an extirpation of awareness.

These similarities should not blind us, however, to the great number of differences in the conceptions of the two men. Jung, for example, saw the Self as having quite an additional phenomenology, as found in many other religions, such as Hinduism and Buddhism, manifesting as geometrical forms (mandalas), and with other properties. Jung's conception, having an empirical and psychological character, was naturally even more "ecumenical", one might say, but these differences are in no way in opposition, as far as I can see. That both men, focussing on the imagination, should arrive at similar ideas and experiences — so far away from the customary modes of apprehension and expression, yet having parallels among formulations of mystics in all religions — is a help to the veridicality of both.

When we come to consider the method of imaginative activity used by these two men, we find much greater dissimilarity. Jung, as is well known, was very much the empirical investigator. Just start with whatever emotionally-laden image arises in fantasy, he would say. Let the fantasy form itself in its own way and then enter into dialogue with it. If one were to follow this empirical method fully, he would imply, one would be likely to encounter all the various figures that he wrote about, namely shadow, anima-animus, old wise-man-woman, mana personality and, finally, the Self. Ibn 'Arabi, on the other hand, begins with the God conception and stays there. That the Sufi mystic also suggests that one bring in a maximum of sensory relaity while undergoing the experience, is similar to Jung's admonition to take imagination totally seriously; only in this way can one truly experience "psychic reality." Jung's method is less prejudical, one might say, in the sense of letting whatever happens happen, but Ibn 'Arabi is equally individual in outlook. The latter's method seems to lie somewhere between "guided imagery" (starting with God) and "active imagination" (honoring the image that arises spontaneously).

For our modern tastes, usually beginning with skepticism and agnosticism, it is probably easier for us to experiment with Jung's method, but it is reassuring that it is not only he who has hit upon individuality as a basic theme. Jung's may be the broader viewpoint for some, but I am impressed that Ibn 'Arabi seems to have found a better solution for "The One and The Many" problem than Jung did (Spiegelman 1989). Jung surely understood the paradox of the opposites in the psyche, and particularly in the symbol of the Self as "one and many," but Ibn 'Arabi, as we have seen, brought these together in a necessary unity. He was even able to cope with the fundamental problem in Islam, when the Lord says, "Thou shalt not see me." He, like the Prophet, also heard those words, yet the communication which followed expressed most profoundly the powerful paradox of those who "know" their own Lord, yet know that they can not "know" the Lord of all. The latter said to him, paradoxically, (p. 379):

> I am myself (unconditioned); you are a determinate self. Do not look for me in yourself, you would be going to futile pains. But do not seek me either outside of you, you would not succeed. Do not renounce looking for me, you would be unhappy. Rather look for me until you find me. Discriminate between me and thee. For you will not see me, you will see only your hexeity (your essential individuality, your Angel or "eye"). Rest therefore in the mode of being in companionship (the divine partner).

The man who could comprehend this mind-breaking paradox also was able to say that it was God:

> who in every beloved being is manifested to the gaze of each lover...and none other than He is adored, for it is impossible to adore a being without conceiving the Godhead in that being...so it is with love: a being does not truly love anyone other than his Creator (p. 146).

This apprehension, so much like the Eros spoken of by Jung in his memoirs, required an experience of the feminine which was remarkable in such strongly patriarchal times. For Ibn 'Arabi, the highest apprehension of God was found in the Feminine, which for him was creative divinity. As was said by another great Islamic mystic, Rumi (p. 163):

> Woman is a beam of the divine Light. She is not the being whom sensual desire takes as its object. She is Creator, it should be said. She is not a Creature.

That these experiences arose out of profound encounters with the feminine, just as it did with Jung, goes without saying. Our present confines do not permit us to describe those experiences, but suffice it to say, that as a consquence of his visions, Ibn 'Arabi formulated a quaternity of the divine in which the feminine was of equal value with the masculine, and it is achieved in a dialectic of love. "Others love you for their own sakes", says the Lord; "I love you for yourself."

References

Corbin, Henry, **Creative Imagination in the Sufism of Ibn 'Arabi,** translated by Ralph Manheim, Bollingen Series, Princeton University Press, Princeton, New Jersey, 1969. (original 1958).

Jung, C.G. **Answer to Job,** (1952) in Collected Works, Vol. XI.

Jung, C.G. "The Transcendent Function" Collected Works, Vol. VIII (1916/1957)

Jung, C.G. **Memories, Dreams, Reflections,** Random House, New York, 1961, 398 pp.

Jung, C.G. **Septem Sermones ad Mortuos,** Watkins, London, 1925 and 1967.

Scholem, Gershom, **Major Trends in Jewish Mysticism,** Schocken, New York, 1941.

Spiegelman, J. Marvin "The One and the Many: Jung and the Post-Jungians", The Journal of Analytical Psychology, January 1989, Vol. 34, No. 1, pp. 53-71.

Dr. Spiegelman is a clinical psychologist (Ph.D., U.C.L.A. 1952), Jungian Analyst (Graduate, C. G. Jung Institute Zurich, 1959) in private practice in the Los Angeles area.

Spiritual Sufi Training Is a Process Of Individuation Leading Into The Infinite

By Irina Tweedie

In his writings C.G. Jung emphasized repeatedly that the process of individuation is purely a psychological and *not* a spiritual one. Consequently, the title of my talk, "Spiritual Sufi training is a process of individuation leading into the infinite" would appear misleading. Still, there are far too many similarities between both of these processes not to allow us to draw significant parallels.

As we all know well, the ultimate goal of individuation is to make a human being whole, complete so to say; in order that all the conscious and the unconscious contents of his psyche may work in unison; the ultimate result should be that he becomes a valid member of human society. The ultimate goal of Sufi training is to live a guided life, guided from within by that which is the Infinite, able to catch the Divine Hint and act accordingly.

From the moment that my Teacher took me seriously in hand, it became increasingly clear to me that the spiritual training was a continuation of the Jungian integration process, but on a higher octave, if I may put it this way. Especially when happenings began to gather momentum, I became more and more fascinated by the discovery that the training devised by the tradition of Yoga thousands of years ago is absolutely identical with certain modern psychological criteria of today.

Jung says — as quoted in *The Way of Individuation* by Jolande Jacobi:

> The experience of God in the form of an encounter or 'unio mystica' is the only possible and authentic way to a genuine belief in God for modern man. The individuation process can 'prepare' a man for such an experience. It can open him to the influence of a world beyond his rational consciousness, and give him insight into it. One might say that in the course of the individuation process a man arrives at the entrance to the house of God.

The Teacher takes the human being further along the way. That is all.

It is not my intention to bore you with the description as to how this is done; all I will try to do is to show you that the Teacher is apt to use the same methods as an analyst — or more correctly, the Teacher will invariably use his yogic powers to help the pupil step by step on the steep ladder of spiritual unfoldment.

How many of us know how the energies work? And how to use them to get the human being exactly to the point needed at this particular moment? I think very, very few.

Every analyst knows about the dangers of inflation. Again and again Jung draws our attention to the danger of being "puffed up".

> The inflation has nothing to do with the *kind* of knowledge, but simply and solely with the fact that any new knowledge can so seize hold of a weak head that he no longer sees and hears anything else. He is hypnotized by it, and instantly believes he has solved the riddle of the universe. But that is equivalent to almighty self-deceit. (Collected Works, Volume 7, p. 243 [footnote])

I often wondered how many Cleopatras and Napoleons are in our mental hospitals because of this inflation turning a weak mind if left unchecked.

Jung himself had had his personal battle with inflation. He tells us in his posthumous work *Memories, Dreams, Reflections*, how, on awakening from a dream in which he killed 'Siegfried', he felt an irresistible urge to fathom out the meaning of the dream which at first eluded him. He knew that his whole future depended on his right understanding of it. It soon dawned on him that he had absolutely to abandon the Siegfried attitude, the arrogance and confidence of the self important ego, for Siegfried was himself, his conscious, cock-sure ego; unless that was completely eliminated it would spell disaster in any confrontation with the unconscious. Commenting upon this Helen Luke remarks:

> Thinking to conquer and mould the forces of the unconscious to his will, Jung himself would most probably have been psychically "killed". In the imagery of Dante, he was in great danger, as he stood on this threshold, of looking upon the Gorgon's head; and so he would have turned to stone, his humanity lost in the coldness of insanity, or despair or uncontrollable inflation. The gate of Dis (a classical name for

the underworld) can only be safely passed by those who have come to the kind of faith and humility which brought the angel to Dante's aid. This Jung knew the moment he understood his dream. ("Dark wood to white rose, a study of meanings in Dante's Divine Comedy", 1975, p. 22)

In my case it was slightly different. The Teacher was there, pointing in the right direction. Here is one example:

A time came when I thought that I was progressing only because much understanding had come to me. One day, on a lovely cool morning, I was sitting in his garden, my Teacher was in his big chair, the beads of his mala (a kind of rosary) were gliding soundlessly through his fingers. Only two or three people were around, immersed in a deep state of *dhyana*. The air was fragrant. A bird was singing in a nearby tree. Slow peaceful thoughts were drifting through my mind.

Suddenly he made a quick movement with his wrist, gathered the mala in his hand and said:

"Why are you trying to become a human being?"

The sudden sentence and the tone of the voice startled me, it was as if he had thrown a ball right into my face.

"Am I not a human being?" I stammered. Could not see what he was driving at...

I stared at his stern, forbidding face.

"Hm," he said. Once more the mala began to glide rhythmically, bead after bead through his slender fingers; and slowly came the words:

"What you are I don't know, but a human being you are not. Only when you will become less than the dust under my feet, only then will you be balanced, only then can you be rightly called a human being."

I went cold. I instantly understood. Of course, inflation, I thought... Merciful God! How on earth did I not see it? Thinking that I was progressing, the moment of elation, of greatness, fleeting feelings of divinity... How dangerous... The word "balanced" gave me the clue. Of course; less than the dust under his feet, in deep humility, how can there be any inflation then?

Boundless was my admiration for him at that moment...

On another occasion when I was complaining a great deal about the excessive suffering to which he was subjecting me, he remarked:

"Your situation was the worst possible one; past karmas are part and parcel of the blood; it all has to be cleared, all of it, otherwise how will you be free?"

The phrase "Unconscious memories are stored in the bloodstream" flashed into my mind. I had read this sentence in Jung's *Memories, Dreams, Reflections.* Here were two identical statements, one by a Yogi who had no idea of modern psychology, and the other by one of the greatest psychiatrists of our time.

I would like to say something about the synchronicity of events which was especially evident when I was with my Teacher.

When my Teacher subjected me to a test I always had the uncanny feeling that there were three of us; my Teacher, myself and a third factor, a "mysterious Something" which one could perhaps call God, or destiny, or could it be a "meaningful coincidence"? And without this third factor the test would be impossible. Each time it happened in such a way that all the circumstances came together, in perfect meaningful order, exactly as it was required by the situation. I will give you one example as to how it worked.

The last two tests at the end of the training are the test of hunger and the test of acceptance of death. I would like to mention the first one, the test of hunger, because in this case the synchronicistic events were really astounding.

To transfer money to India via bank draft took about six weeks. I had found out that if I sent to my friend in London a cheque on my bank, she would cash it and make out a postal order of the same amount addressed to me in India; then the whole transaction would take only three to four days. That is how we did it and I received my pension regularly this way. Now, it happened that my friend in London had builders repairing a wall in her house and she was also otherwise busy and not being able to go to the Post office personally, she asked an acquaintance of hers to do it for her, and to send the amount by registered air mail to my address in India. The woman did send the money registered, but by sea mail, which takes six weeks. I was waiting and waiting for the money to arrive, not understanding why it did not come...I was reduced to eating only potatoes, then the peelings of the potatoes left over, and after that, only water to drink. The attitude of my Teacher gave me a clear indication that he was subjecting me to a test.

I thought that I passed this test and I told him so a few weeks afterwards. He only laughed and changed the subject.

And it was always so; the circumstances arranged themselves in such a way that not only tests, but the whole of my life, were regulated by them to a far more obvious degree than happens ordinarily.

At that time it was a great mystery to me; I did not understand it. Now when more than twenty years have passed and with the knowledge I have acquired, it seems to me that there is really nothing to understand, it is all quite natural. Coincidences do not exist, all is part of the Wholeness, ourselves, our environment, our state of mind, everything! Subjected to an unusual psychological pressure as I was, my own psyche created the necessary conditions at that particular moment.

Anyone of us who has had at least a glimpse of the interlinkedness that underlies all things in the universe; or, to put it differently, anyone who has had the experience of the absolute one-ness of all life, of causation, transition, time, space, in one word, anyone who has embraced the whole as one glorious chord resounding forever in eternity, such a one, I think, might get at least an idea of how it works.

The *Upanishads* tell us:

> Brahma before you, Brahma behind you, Brahma above and below you,
> Brahma to the right and to the left, and there is nothing else but Brahma.

and

> It is outside and inside you and you cannot see it, nor touch it, nor smell it, but you can realise it, if you desire realisation.

Similarly says the *Bhagavad Gita*:

> I am the beginning, the middle and also the end of all beings (10.20)
> Nor is there aught, moving or unmoving, that may exist bereft of me. (10.39)

And Saint Paul said (I quote from memory): "Like fish in water we are in Him and have our being."

Perhaps we can grasp this intellectually; but then it means little. Only if it is for us a living experience, a widening of our horizon, without frontiers, without borders, loosing ourselves into the endlessness, then and only then could we understand. It is said somewhere, "like the dewdrop slipping into the shining sea." I would rather put it, "like the shining sea flowing into the dew drop." And you feel yourself flowing out like a river, flowing out endlessly without ever diminishing... It is the most one can say, it is impossible for the mind to grasp it entirely, nor can one express it adequately in words.

On this subject C.G. Jung in volume 8 of his *Collected Works*, quotes Pico della Mirandola:

Firstly there is the unity in things whereby each thing is at one with itself, consists of itself, and coheres with itself. Secondly, there is the unity whereby one creature is united with the others and all parts of the world constitute one world. The third and most important (unity) is that whereby the whole universe is one with the Creator, as an army with its commander. (Heptaplus VI proem, in Opera omnia, Basel 1557, p. 40; Jung, *Collected Works*, Volume 8, pp. 490-1.)

Jung comments thus:

For him the world is One being, a visible God, in which everything is naturally arranged from the very beginning like the parts of a living organism. The world appears as the Corpus Mysticum of God...Just as in a living body the different parts work in harmony and are meaningfully adjusted to one another, so events in the world stand in a meaningful relationship which cannot be derived from any immanent causality. The reason for this is that in either case the behaviour of the parts depends on a central control which is supraordinate to them. (*Collected Works*, Volume 8, p. 491)

In fact Jung defines *synchronicity* as a "meaningful coincidence". All happens within the oneness, that Oneness which Plotinus, the greatest of the Neo-Platonic School of philosophy, described thus:

For there (in the oneness) everything is transparent, nothing dark, nothing resistant: every being is lucid to every other, in breadth and depth, light runs through light. And each of them contains all within itself, and at the same time sees all in every other, so that everywhere there is all, all is all, and each all, and infinte the glory. Each of them is great; the small is great; the sun, there, is all the stars, and every star again is all the stars and sun..." (Ennead, V. 8)

As one proceeds on the path of Spirituality one realises more and more the meaningful relation of the One to its parts. I think the secret is to see the detail as part of the whole.

What is the inner mechanism of synchronicity? How does it work?

It works by mirroring, by reflection. Everything mirrors itself into everything else. We are exposed to impressions from morning to evening from everyone with whom we come into contact.

At this moment my mind mirrors itself into your mind and your mind into my mind. It helps me to speak to you and it helps you to understand what I am talking about. Only, in reality, the understanding does not depend on speech; it is the atmosphere that matters. Speech, language, are external means by which we communicate with each other at the mental level, but the natural communication is this reflection which is mirrored from one to another.

For instance, if we are with peaceful people we feel peaceful, the aura of peace is around them. If we are among restless people, or gloomy people, we will feel restless or gloomy; one does not even need to speak to another or show one's gloom, everyone can feel it.

Very often we develop the attribute belonging to the object which we hold in our thought. Reflection always works unconsciously but one can become aware of it and influence it with the conscious mind. We will be that which has come from the impression that we have received from someone else. We must not forget how creative the mind is. If you think of failure, failure will be attracted to you and you will fail constantly whatever you do. If there is anything that is reflected in our mind, we reflect it in outer life; and every sphere that our heart has touched is charged with the heart's impression. As my teacher said:

> What is in the heart becomes expressed outwardly. The exterior reflects the inner attitude. (*Daughter of Fire*, p. 222)

The *Upanishads* tell us that what one thinks, that one becomes; it is true; we become identified with the object of our thought; it becomes our own property, our own quality. Therefore the *Upanishads* add: Meditate on God.

After the death of my Teacher, when I was in the solitude of the Himalayan hills undergoing an inner transformation, even Nature around me reflected my state of mind; the storms, the cloud capped peaks, the mists, the rainbows, the incredibly still nights full of stars, so near; all of it nearly always reflected what I felt within. And I was perfectly aware of the fact that it was not I reflecting happenings around myself; no; it was Nature mirroring outwardly what was happening within myself.

The mind becomes more and more one-pointed like an arrow pointing to its target. Very powerful is the one-pointed mind. The mind of every human being is powerful, but the mind aimed directly towards its goal is omnipotent.

"Unto the Eternal verily shall he go who, in his action reflects wholly upon the Eternal" says the Bhagavad Gita (4.24).

One has to be careful how one thinks because that which we have thought actually becomes! Here lies the explanation of the so-called miracles and wonder-working. These are nothing else but the very one-pointed mind at work.

Synchronicity is a fact. Chance does not exist. Cannot exist; it only looks to us, in our ignorance, like chance. It only looks thus to those of us who do not know the inner workings of the Law.

At the time when the darkness in me was rapidly coming up and the worst in my character was being brought out and had to be faced — otherwise how would it be possible to go ahead on the way my Teacher was leading me? — he would switch off my mind; yes switch it off, I mean it literally. His repeated assertions that this path is effortless only served to increase my rebellion. Did I not know how much and how great an effort it cost me? But he was right. It is effortless. What is given is an act of Grace; a gift; how can a gift be an act of effort on the part of the one who receives it? The effort lies somewhere else..."in the power or endurance, the capacity for sacrifice, the will to go on, to hold out at any cost..." (*Daughter of Fire*, p. 194) One has to be worthy of the Grace. The cup has to be cleaned and emptied.

So from time to time my Teacher switched off my mind, the result being that the mind would work to a quarter of its strength or half according as it was switched off, twenty-five percent, or fifty percent or sometimes even seventy-five percent. In the latter case one could hardly think. It was never done for a long time; one cannot live without the mind! It was done to help me so that the quality of the Higher Principle, the spiritual insight, could come through, otherwise the mind clutters the channel of communication with its restless modifications.

The state of mindlessness is quite painless and very peaceful; one just cannot think. That is all.

The world around me became so lovely, full of light, a strange luminosity, a kind of elevated feeling, of special meaning. But it was also quite bewildering. Two very important factors were:

1. Firstly, the restricted physical vision. When it happens one cannot see except right in front as if one had blinkers such as are seen on horses. Also if I tried to look sideways turning my eyes either to the right or to the left, I became giddy.

2. Secondly, the mind itself, the thinking process would work in a kind of slow motion. To give an example: When leaving my Teacher's garden where I usually sat, and walking down the street to go to my small Indian-style dwelling, all I could do was to be careful where to put my feet and watch the traffic, the crazy traffic of an Indian street. Cycles, rickshaws dashing along furiously ringing their bells non stop,

cows wandering about aimlessly, chickens darting in and out between all and everything, taxis weaving about to avoid dogs and rickshaws and pedestrians, and hooting wildly, and I just able to look straight ahead, hardly taking anything in, only vaguely conscious of my surroundings.

To go home was a rather complicated undertaking. My Indian style accommodation consisted of a small courtyard round a tiny kitchen, a shower and a toilet cubicle, a small veranda and two small rooms opening onto the veranda. All surrounded by a nine foot wall which made it very private. To judge by Indian standards it was a very nice flat.

Arrived at the narrow door leading to the courtyard, I would stop. A door...it must be my door...It is familiar, so it must be mine. I kept thinking. To open it I would need a key. A key...a key...Ah! yes, in my bag...I began to rummage my bag in search of the key. Found it...Put it into the keyhole, opened and closed the door behind me. Kept standing at the door...Am hungry...If hungry I must eat...eat...eat...What? I did not remember what I had at home. I stared in front of me at the kitchen which had no door, was open to all elements. See some potatoes on the shelf. Stare at the potatoes. At first do not register what they are...Oh, yes, potatoes. Potatoes one has to cook...To cook them one has to peel them. To peel...to peel. Oh yes, one needs a knife...a knife, a knife...I keep looking at the knife before I am able to understand what it is. When I realise that it is what I want, I can begin to peel the potatoes. And so it went on with every action, with every thought. Everything was very much slowed down, for when I looked at things it took time to understand what they were, or what they were for, and what to do with them, and what the next action should be.

Life becomes rather complicated, but as I said it never lasted too long. Never longer than half a day and sometimes only for a few hours. And it is painless, as I have already mentioned.

When back in London, I was giving a lecture and explaining all that I have just said here. At the end of my talk a Canadian psychiatrist, who happened to be in the audience, asked me if I knew what was happening. I did not know; all I knew was that my Teacher was switching off my mind.

"Those symptoms you were describing," explained the psychiatrist, "are symptoms of schizophrenia. Thinking in slow motion, tunnel vision above all, sensation of light, of brilliance, of unreality. Your Teacher was creating an artificial schizophrenia. When a human being is standing with both feet firmly on the ground, with both legs on this earth, he is 'quite normal' as we medical practitioners call it, spiritual life is very difficult, perhaps even impossible. But if something is not quite right in the mind, a little wheel not properly working in the clockwork of the mind, then spiritual life is easy."

We in the West have no idea of what the spiritual life implies in reality. Spiritual life is hard and rough, it means that one is taken into the arena, to fight one's ultimate battle...The Master who knows his job will make one bite the dust; training is an analysis "plus", in the sense that yogic power is used to bring the human being to the "cooking point", at the maturity point the Teacher wants him to be.

> For the self will not go in gladness and with caresses; it must
> be chased with sorrow, drowned in tears...(a Persian song)

When my Teacher sent me back to London in the spring of 1963 his wish was that I should lecture. When I asked him what he wanted me to speak on: "About Sufism, of course," he answered. I had never lectured in my life before. I knew hardly anything about Sufism when I came to him, and I felt he taught me practically nothing. I told him so. I had a smattering of Hindu Scriptures, knew something about Hindu philosophy, but Sufism is different and I was puzzled. "If you are in despair you will cry for help and...it is always there."

I had to be content with that.

In England many people knew that I had been in India with a Teacher, so it happened that I was asked to talk about India, about my Teacher and as the time went on, I found myself speaking on all sorts of subjects.

Later, when I had the opportunity to read some Sufi books I found that on whatever subject I happened to lecture, the point of view I presented was always the Sufi point of view. I wrote about it to my Teacher, but in his few letters to me he never commented on it. This, however, was not unusual; as a rule he explained very little to us.

After the death of my Teacher I stayed for a few months in a Vedic Sadhak Ashram in North India, near Dehra Dun. Twice a day a fire ceremony was performed with the chanting of the sacred Gayatri mantra. In the lovely, warm evenings, at dusk, I had interesting discussions with the learned, orange-robed swamis. Many spoke good English. I talked a lot about my Teacher who had died so recently. I felt so bereft. Once I happened to mention in conversation the fact that though I knew nothing about Sufism, its philosphy, its metaphysics, somehow it seemed to be quite naturally part of my mind as if I always knew it.

"Oh yes," said one of the swamis, "It is *hirdambara buddhi*; the knowledge which is not learned, it is reflected into the tranquil mind of a yogi when the animal tendencies of like and dislike have ceased to be."

I must confess, I did not particularly think that my mind was all that tranquil, but after all a certain amount of yogic detachment must have been achieved after being several years with my Teacher.

There exists a knowledge which is not learned. It is infused, or rather reflected directly into the mind from another plane of being. As everything in the universe is relected from the Inner plan, the Unmanifested plane into the plane of Manifestation, so knowledge can also be directly reflected into the mind of an individual. The *Upanishads* have a beautiful symbolic expression for this:

> Under the banyan tree sits the boy teacher amidst his aged disciples.
> Silent remains the Teacher, and all the doubts of the disciples dissolve.

Through the tranquil pool of his mind the disciple learns to reflect the mind of his teacher, to catch his hint and finally to catch the Divine Hint. As my Teacher himself put it:

> First one learns how to catch the hint of the guru, and afterwards, when one is well merged, the Divine Hint, which is faster than lightning. The guru will hint first; if the hint is not understood, then he orders. An order is easy to understand, but the guru trains the disciple to catch the Divine Hint rather. The guru can give orders again and again if the disciple does not understand; but God does not do so and the Hint is lost, and one may wait for a long time to get it again.
> To grasp it one must be deeply merged, so merged that one even looks for a place to stand upon, but there seems to be none.
> To grasp the hint is to act accordingly, and not even try to understand it. Acting accordingly is necessary rather than understanding. The Grace of God cannot be seized; it descends.

All of us must have seen the old black and white film of Carl Jung being interviewed by a journalist of the B.B.C. In it Jung is asked if he believes in God and his answer is: "I don't believe; I know." In the same film towards the end Carl Jung says: "Trust the meaning and make the meaning your Goal."

I think this is the message to humanity for centuries to come. It does not matter whether the meaning be to become a successful greengrocer —

or to realize the Truth. It is the Meaning which makes the whole of life worth while.

Yes; to trust the meaning and to make it the goal; and the world thereby could be changed.

This paper was presented to the VIII International Conference of the International Transpersonal Association at Davos, Switzerland, September 1st, 1983.

Irina Tweedie was born in Russia in 1907 and educated in Vienna and Paris. Following World War II she married an English naval officer, whose death in 1954 started her on a spiritual quest. A friend introduced her to Theosophy, and she worked as a librarian at the Theosophical Society in London, during which time she studied the works of Carl Jung in depth. At the age of 52 she travelled to India, where she met a Sufi Master, who ordered her to keep a diary of her spiritual training. After his death in 1966 she returned to London, and her diaries were eventually published, first in an abridged form as *Chasm of Fire*, and then finally unabridged, as *Daughter of Fire* (Blue Dolphin Publishing, Nevada City, 1986). During her time with her Teacher she noticed many similarities between her Sufi training and Jung's process of individuation.

Dream-Work Within A Sufi Tradition

By Llewellyn Vaughn-Lee

For Sufis, dreams have always been considered as important, offering guidance along the spiritual path. Early Sufi manuals have sections on dreams, and an autobiographical sketch[1] by the ninth century Sufi saint, al-Hakim al-Tirmidhi, records many of the dreams that helped guide him, some of which he states as being too obvious to need any interpretation. Interestingly, he also describes dreams that his wife had for him, where she played the part of a "messenger". In one such dream she was shown a dry tree, with withered branches, springing out of a rocky barren land. A bird then appeared and, alighting on the tree commenced to hop from branch to branch. Wherever the bird touched the tree, green leaves and bunches of grapes appeared. However, she was given the message that the tree must be looked after, otherwise the bird would not be able to go to the topmost branches, but only half way up the tree. Grapes are a powerful Sufi symbol, because from the grape is made the wine of the Beloved that intoxicates the Sufi. Thus al-Tirmidhi is told to look after the tree of his life and teachings, so that the bird of divine inspiration could fully transform it, and produce grapes to nourish the souls of those who lived in a spiritually barren land.

The twelfth century Sufi, Najmuddin Kubra (1145-1220) stressed the importance of dreams and their interpretation, including in the rules of the Path, along with "constant silence, constant retreat and constant recollection of God", "constant direction of a sheikh who explains the meaning of one's dreams and visions".[2] In this century, in *Daughter of Fire*, Irina Tweedie gives a contemporary autobiographical account of a

---

[1] Bad'u al-Sha'n (The Beginning of My Story) ed. Uthman Yahya (Beirut, 1965).

[2] Annemarie Schimmel, *Mystical Dimensions of Islam* (Chapel Hill, 1975) p.225.

spiritual training with a Sufi Master, who regarded her dreams as
offering important guidance. He ordered her to keep a diary:

> I would like you to keep a diary, day-by-day entries of all
> your experiences. And also to keep a record of your dreams. Your
> dreams you must tell me, and I will interpret them for you.
> Dreams are important; they are a guidance.[3]

Daughter of Fire records many of Irina Tweedie's dreams, some of
which are interpreted, for example the following dream which images
the slow process of becoming nothing before God:

> DREAM: I was looking at myself in a mirror and saw that I was very
> thin, very pale, my hair in disorder.
> INTERPRETATION: "It is a very good dream! Thin and thinner until
> nothing will remain."[4]

But other dreams are not interpreted, sometimes because it was not
appropriate to give the meaning at that time, and sometimes, as with
al-Tirmidhi, because their meaning is quite clear, as when she dreamt
that she was in a hospital and her heart was being examined by a
doctor with a stethoscope. To this dream her Teacher responded:
"Interpretation is not needed. The symbology is quite clear: your heart
is being examined."[5]

The Sufi Master in *Daughter of Fire* belongs to the Naqshbandi
Mujaddidia Dynasty, the Indian branch of the Naqshbandi Sufis. The
Naqshbandi, named after Baha a Din Naqshband (died 1390), are also
called the Silent Sufis, because they practise silent meditation. Unlike
other Sufi Schools they practise the recollection of the heart with no
ceremonies, no ritual, no music, no sacred dancing. In this paper I would
like to explore how dreams and their interpretation function within a
Naqshbandi group which I have attended for the last fifteen years. At
the group meetings individuals are encouraged to tell their dreams,
which are then interpreted within the group. The dreamer benefits by
sharing his/her dream and coming to understand its meaning. The
others also benefit by participating in the experience and learning
about the spiritual path and the dynamics of the psyche as explored
through the dream. All are encouraged to offer interpretations which
both presents the dreamer with a variety of perspectives on the dream

---

[3] Irina Tweedie, *Daughter of Fire* (Nevada City, 1986) p. 12.
[4] ibid. p. 157.
[5] ibid. p. 113.

and gives the opportunity for others to develop their sensitivity and intuitive understanding of dreams. This dream-work is considered as the modern equivalent of the ancient Sufi teaching stories.

The dream-work within this group has a strong Jungian orientation. This reflects the similarities between the spiritual training in this Sufi System and the Jungian process of individuation. The practice of silent meditation of the heart has the effect of energizing the psyche so that its contents are brought into consciousness. In particular, the individual is brought face to face with the darkness within, with the "Shadow". As Irina Tweedie comments:

> I had hoped to get instructions in Yoga, expected wonderful teachings, but what the Teacher did was mainly to force me to face the darkness within myself, and it almost killed me.

> In other words he made me "descend into hell," the cosmic drama enacted in every soul as soon as it dares lift its face to the Light.[6]

For Irina Tweedie it was the yogic powers of her Teacher which evoked her inner darkness in a dramatic and often terrifying manner. For most Wayfarers on this Path the unconscious, activated through meditation, is experienced more gradually. Nonetheless, the individual follows the same path, first into the world of the personal shadow, and then into deeper archetypal realms.

The importance of Jung's work is that, within the field of modern psychology, he has most fully charted this inner mythic quest and understood the Reality of the Self that is its goal. In particular, in *Mysterium Coniunctionis* Jung describes in rich symbolic detail the psychological dynamics of the spiritual path toward wholeness. Jungian psychology thus offers an invaluable means for the Western mind to understand, as far as possible, the psychological processes encountered on the Path. For example, in Sufi texts there is a prolific occurrence of pairs of opposites, (e.g. *qurb* [nearness] and *bu'd* [separation]), which "refer to psychological states or stages of the Sufi on his way to spiritual realization".[7] Thus the Sufi is thrown, often violently, between these opposites, a phenomenon which has been termed in our group as the "Yo-Yo Syndrome". This process, which is

---

[6] ibid. p. x.

[7] Sara Sviri, "Between Fear and Hope. On the Coincidence of Opposites in Islamic Mysticism", *Jerusalem Studies for Arabic and Islam* 9, 1987, p. 321.

experienced by everyone on the Path, is a continual fluctuation between up and down: one day you feel wonderful and meditation goes very well, then the next day you feel awful, you feel that you are not progressing at all, and meditation seems hopeless. In *Mysterium Coniunctionis* Jung offers a psychological explanation for this phenomenon, describing it as the reconciliation of opposites:

> Ascent and descent, above and below, up and down, represent an emotional realization of opposites, and this realization gradually leads, or should lead, to their equilibrium. This motif occurs very frequently in dreams, in the form of going up- and downhill, climbing stairs, going up or down in a lift, balloon, aeroplane etc....As Dorn interprets it, this vacillating between the opposites and being tossed back and forth means being contained *in* the opposites. They become a vessel in which what was previously now one thing and now another floats vibrating, so that the painful suspension between opposites gradually changes into the bilateral activity of the point in the centre. This is the "liberation from opposites," the *nirdvandva* of Hindu philosophy, though it is not really a philosophical development.[8]

This is but one instance of Jung offering an invaluable comment on a psychological process that is an integral part of the Sufi Path.

However, it is also necessary to acknowledge the limitations of Jungian Psychology in relation to the Sufi Path. For, while psychology aims to understand the dynamics of the psyche, the aim of the Sufi is to transcend individual consciousness in a mystical union with the Beloved, or God. Jung's description of the *unio mystica* in itself suggests the limitations of a psychological perspective:

> that absolute reality where one is nothing but psychic reality, yet confronted with the psychic reality that one is not...The ego disappears completely. The psychical is no longer a content in us, but we become contents of it...this condition...is almost unimaginable.[9]

Thus the Sufi Path both embraces and looks beyond Jungian Psychology, and this will be reflected in any Sufi dream-work. For

---

[8] C. G. Jung *Collected Works, Vol. 14, Mysterium Coniunctionis* para. 296. (Collected Works of C.G. Jung, published by Routledge and Kegan Paul, London)

[9] C. G. Jung, "Commentary on Kundalini Yoga". *Spring* 1976 p. 17.

example, an understanding of Jungian symbolism needs to be combined with an awareness of the Sufi symbols that image the mystical dynamics of the Path.

In this paper I would like to focus on dream-work that combines a Jungian and a Sufi perspective. First, before interpreting any dream it is necessary to know "from where the dream comes".[10] There are different types of dreams, which will each require a different approach. Beside psychological dreams there are "mind dreams" in which the mind reviews previous events. There are prophetic dreams and also dreams of past-lives. There are dreams which are for others, as with those of the wife of al-Tirmidhi, and then there are dreams which are in fact not dreams at all, but experiences on another plane of consciousness. For when the body is asleep the soul is free, "the king is not in his castle, the prisoner is not in his cell", and there are other planes of existence beside the physical world. Teaching is often given in such dreams: al-Tirmidhi had a dream in which he was shown a chair in the desert and told "This will lead you to God", and in our group someone dreamt of being at the *Satsang* (sitting in the presence of the Teacher) of our Teacher's Teacher, who then showed a film of himself as a young man, flying a kite, teaching that in spiritual life one can only "fly high" if one's feet are firmly on the ground.

Dreams on First Coming to the Group

Most frequently guidance is offered through psychological dreams, and these guiding dreams are the main concern of this paper. Such guidance is often given from the moment the individual comes to our group. Jung observed that when the unconscious notices that something is to be done about it, it will respond with a dream or series of dreams. Often just before or after a person first comes to our group, they will have an important dream, one that may point out the direction of his/her spiritual path and the psychological work that needs to be done. The following dream, which the dreamer told when she first came, describes her path in a series of symbolic images:

> I am walking on a tightrope. A man with a long fork comes and tries to get me down, but I take the fork from him and use it as a balancing pole. Then a pair of hands takes my shoulders, and like a trapeze artist I swing round and round. Then I fly through the air and come to a green fountain; I go through the fountain, underwater. I am happy underwater, and don't need to

---

10 Irina Tweedie, op. cit. p. 560.

breathe, it is as if I breathe through gills. Then I am a fish and there is the figure of Neptune with a three pronged fork, he spears me. I come to in a field with pain in three chakras. I put leaves on the pain. A small man comes and puts a gold ring around my left foot. On the ring is written "God helps those who help themselves". Then I am a buffalo in a herd of buffaloes, suddenly I feel a searing pain in my shoulder as I am being branded. I am in MacDonalds, eating a hamburger, and the smell is the same as the herd of buffaloes. I can't eat the hamburger and vomit.

A full appreciation of this dream would require an essay in itself, but in our dream-work we tend to focus on those aspects that are most spiritually significant. The spiritual path is often imaged as a tightrope or narrow bridge. A famous Zen picture by Hakuin, "Blind Men Crossing a Bridge"[11] shows the Path as a narrow bridge over a chasm, over which three blind men are slowly groping their way. The seeker must walk "on the razor's edge", always keeping an inner balance, and an early Christian mystic, Saint Gregory of Nyssa (c. 331-396), describes the Path of Love as "a Bridge of Hair Across a Chasm of Fire". In the above dream, while the dreamer is walking on a tightrope, the shadow, in the form of Satan, "A man with a long fork", tries to upset her balance. Only too often does this happen on the Path, as the shadow pulls us down, and time and again we fall. But here the dreamer takes the fork and uses it as a "balancing pole". This is a profound statement on how the shadow can in fact help us, offering insight into our inner nature, and indeed, allow us to become "more balanced".

Lifted and swung round, the dreamer is in the hands of God. Flying through the air she goes underwater, and the fact that she is happy there and doesn't need to breathe shows how she is at home in the unconscious. As a fish she becomes at one with her unconscious nature, when she is speared, not by Satan, but by Neptune, Lord of the Sea. Neptune could here symbolize the divine aspect of the animus,[12] especially as she "comes to" on dry land. It is the animus who helps the woman leave the waters of her own unconscious self for the land of consciousness, though any such process of conscious awareness can often be painful, as imaged by the "pain in the three chakras". This pain is

---

[11] Yasuichi Awakawa, *Zen Painting* (Tokyo, 1970) p. 125 & 6.

[12] C. G. Jung *Collected Works Vol. 12, Psychology and Alchemy* plate 132.

healed through relating again to the natural world, "leaves". The "Gold ring around my left foot" has a profound Sufi symbolism. Slaves often had rings placed around their ankles, and Sufis are the "slaves of God" ("slaves of the One and servants of the many"). The ring is gold, symbolizing the transformation inherent in this slavery, and it also suggests the image of a wedding ring, for the Sufi is married to the Beloved. The fact that the ring is around the left foot implies that this whole process takes place through the unconscious, which is a part of the feminine mystery of the surrender to God.

The saying, "God helps those who help themselves", needs no interpretation, but the branding of the buffalo is highly symbolic. The buffalo is similar to the "ox" of the Zen "Oxherding Pictures", which as Spiegelman comments, is the Self, "the divine itself."[13] The dreamer as a buffalo symbolizes that she is at one with her whole divine instinctual Self; and it is as a buffalo, as her divine Nature, that she is branded by God. There are those who are branded by God, they belong only to him, and this is echoed in a saying attributed to Christ: "I know my sheep and my sheep know me." For those who are so branded, this world only has meaning as a path to Him. Significantly, when she is branded, ordinary life — a hamburger at MacDonalds — is very difficult to digest, it makes her sick. Yet the dream also shows how, in fact, this world — imaged as a hamburger which reflects the smell and the meat of the buffalo — embodies God's instinctual Self. At first, when one has seen through the illusion of the world and glimpsed the beyond, physical existence becomes distasteful. But later, all becomes one and there is no sense of duality between the Creator and the creation. This is imaged in the final Oxherding picture, when the old man goes to the market: "He is found in company with winebibbers and butchers, he and they are all converted into Buddhas."[14]

While the above dream images the Sufi as a slave of God, the following dream describes the spiritual path as freeing the dreamer from the chains of this world. It was dreamt by a man soon after he first came to our group:

> I am on an island full of people drinking, laughing etc., but I know that a great storm and tidal wave is coming, so I go to a hill in the middle of the island and climb a tree. The storm comes and all the people are killed, but I just hang on and

---

[13] M. Spiegelman *Buddhism and Jungian Psychology* (Phoenix, 1985) p. 60.

[14] ibid. p. 79.

survive. Then after the storm a pirate ship comes to the island and takes me off as a slave, though I ask not to be chained, and the pirates agree. They take me to a port where there is a slave market; all the other slaves are chained but they are paper chains. The paper chains then catch fire, and burn, but no one is hurt.

The dream begins with the dreamer as part of the concourse of life, "people drinking, laughing". This is the world of material existence, and yet it is on an island, suggesting that for the dreamer it embodies a certain isolation: he is isolated from his real self. But a storm and tidal wave is coming: embarking on the spiritual path will bring a storm, a great inner disturbance that will destroy these people, and leave the dreamer all alone. How often is this experienced by those who begin the spiritual quest, worldly values and pursuits become empty and friends drop away, leaving one feeling alone. The door of this world closes behind you, and yet the next door has not yet opened. Rescued by a pirate ship the dreamer becomes a slave, though not chained. This image of a slave could refer to the dreamer becoming a slave of God, but the idea of slavery and chains also suggests another meaning. Whilst most people in the world think that they are free, one of the first things the seeker discovers on the Path are the chains of desire and conditioning that imprison him, and indeed the Arabic word for a human being, *'abd*, also carries the meaning of slave. One cannot become truly free until one has become aware that one is chained, and paradoxically, only those who become slaves of God are really free, free from the chains of the *nafs* or ego.

When the dreamer is taken to the slave market he sees that all the other slaves are chained "but they are paper chains." The chains of this world can be burnt away only by the desire for Truth, and this is what happens. Significantly, when these chains burn, the slaves are not burnt. The fire that burns but does not burn has great spiritual significance, echoing the fire in the burning bush of Moses. This is the purifying fire of God, that burns away the dross, the chains of this world. Thus this dream describes the unfolding of the dreamer's spiritual path, on which, as a slave, he is freed from chains that are made only of paper.

Alchemical Transformation

Once the seeker is on the Path, the process of alchemical transformation takes place, fueled by aspiration and meditation. Although one's spiritual journey is always a solitary path — it is the journey "from the alone to the Alone" — on the Sufi Path one is in the hands of a Teacher and in the company of other Wayfarers, as is imaged in the following dream:

> The group is at a school for turning base metal into silver. We all at first try, sweeping up the earth and finding bits of silver in it. We have to make silver bowls. Then when we have done this for a while a man tells the secret of the process, which is that the silver must be rolled out five times, and then moulded from above and below into the shape of a bowl.

The alchemical process turns base matter, lead, into gold, and Sufis have often used alchemical terminology to describe the stages of inner transformation, as for example in *The Alchemy of Happiness* by al-Ghazali (died 1111). In this dream the "base metal" is being turned into silver, which is significant in that silver is symbolically feminine, and the Sufi Path is feminine; for it is the longing, the feminine side of love, the cup waiting to be filled, that takes the Sufi to God. This cup is the "silver bowl" of the dream, which must be made in the workshop of the heart.

The dream's image of "sweeping up the earth" evokes the idea of the *prima materia*, which must be found before the alchemical process can commence. The *prima materia* is that which is rejected and considered waste:

> This Matter lies before the eyes of all; everybody sees it, touches it, loves it, but knows it not. It is glorious and vile, precious and of small account, and is found everywhere.[15]

From a psychological perspective the work of transformation begins with the shadow, the parts of oneself that are rejected and undervalued. But "sweeping" also has a specific Sufi symbolism, for Sufis are known as "sweepers" or the "dustbins of humanity". In one dream, Irina Tweedie met a Great Sufi with his followers, and when she asked a disciple if he was a Bishop she was told:

> "No, no...he is on the same line as Bhai Sahib (Irina Tweedie's Teacher) and he is very fond of joking; speaking of himself and those like him, he will say: 'Nous autres balayeurs'" (which means in French: 'we sweepers').

---

15 Waite trans., *The Hermetic Museum* 1:13, quoted by E. Edinger *Anatomy of the Psyche* La Salle, Illinois, 1985) p. 11.

"Oh, I see!" I exclaimed, "it is because they clean the hearts
of people!"

"Precisely!" the disciple said.[16]

The idea of the Sufi as a "dustbin" was reflected in a dream told in
our group:

I had two dustbins full of rubbish. the Teacher came along
and emptied my two dustbins into his one dustbin, and walked
off.

In this dream of turning base metal into silver, a teacher figure "tells
the secret of the process, which is that the silver must be rolled out five
times, and then moulded from above and below into the shape of a
bowl." That the silver must be rolled out five times is very significant,
for five is the number of mankind or humanity: we have five senses; and
in order to fully realize an inner transformation it must be lived. This is
reflected in the fact that, according to Jung, the final stage in an
alchemical process is the "reddening".

In order to come alive it must have "blood", it must have
what the alchemists call the rubedo, the "redness" of life.[17]

On the Sufi path this "reddening" is effected through being "in the
world but not of the world". A central feature of the Naqshbandi Path
is "Solitude in the Crowd":

Rather than shunning away from earthly duties, or choosing
an ascetic and monastic Path, the Naqshbandi teachers teach
their disciples how to be involved in life without being
attached to its values. One has to marry, to bring up a family,
to go into the market place as a craftsman or a merchant, in
short to be totally undistinguished, just one of the crowd. Yet at
the same time one has to keep the fire of the internal journey
kindled, as well as devotion to the Teacher, the Spiritual
Guide, and the longing of the heart.[18]

In this way the silver is rolled five times, and the bowl moulded by
the grace of God from above, and by the experience of world, from
below.

---

[16] Irina Tweedie, op. cit. p. 345.

[17] C. G. Jung *C. G. Jung Speaking* p. 229 quoted by E. Edinger op. cit. p.
147.

[18] Sara Sviri Unpublished paper on the Naqshmandi Path.

In another dream, the *prima materia* is imaged in a more ordinary, everyday context: again there is the figure of the Teacher helping the dreamer:

> I am in a room where there has been a party. There is a box full of all the left-overs from the party, crusts of bread, etc. My Teacher tells me to eat the left-overs, but I don't know how to begin. I look at the box and think how can I eat all these things. My Teacher takes the box and a paper plate and arranges some of the left-overs in a nice pattern on the plate, and begins to eat — she shows how simple it is.

In this dream the *prima materia* is what is "left-over" from the party of life. It is something undervalued and overlooked, rejected and considered inedible, which the higher Self, personified as the Teacher, shows to be part of a pattern and so edible. Furthermore, "she shows how simple it is", for spiritual life is in itself very simple, it is only the mind which complicates.

The spiritual Path, like the Alchemical Opus, takes the seeker into the very depths of the psyche. The process of transformation takes place not only in the personal unconscious, the "shadow", but in the realm of the archetypes. In the following dream the dreamer, a woman, encounters the Goddess, and yet is apprehensive of her power:

> I am in a circus, in the arena. There is a central post which holds up the tent. Many people from the group are moving around the post, like in a merry-go-round. Then I see a woman who is very, very beautiful, the most beautiful woman I have ever seen. She has stars on her ears and fingers. She is called Maria. Then in the middle of the arena there are some tigers. Maria and a male member of the group are quite happy playing with the tigers. Then the tigers go outside; but after a while they come back and I have to let them in. I see them first through a glass wall and am a bit apprehensive.

The dreamer meets the Goddess Maria in the circus arena, under the tent. The tent and its central post are ancient Sufi symbols, for the sheikh is the post, the link between heaven and earth which provides a protected space for the disciples to come closer to God. The arena is also a powerful symbol, for the Sufi, once committed to the Path, is taken into the arena to do battle with the *nafs*. And the words of the Roman gladiators, *Ave, Imperator, morituri te salutant*, ('Hail, Emperor, those about to die salute you') are appropriate to the Sufi, for in that arena the ego is to die, reflecting a tradition ascribed to the prophet, that one has to die before one dies. This "death" is not the obliteration of the ego, for one cannot live in this world without it. Only in the states of *Samadhi*, in the *unio mystica*, does "the ego disappear completely." But in the arena, the ego is dissolved and transformed so that it remains constantly surrendered to the higher Self and to God. Yet for the disciple this transformation is experienced as a death, a painful process of dying to this world and its desires, in order that one may fully awaken to the presence of the Beloved.

There, in the arena, the dreamer meets the Great Goddess, known in the West as Maria or the Virgin Mary. "The most beautiful woman I have ever seen," she is adorned with stars, reflecting her archetypal nature, and she is playing with tigers. The tiger is the vehicle of the Goddess,[19] and it is often associated with her dark side, the Terrible Goddess. The tiger represents her power, her undifferentiated primordial energy, which is the aspect of the Goddess most repressed in our patriarchal culture. This primal feminine power, which is emphasized by there being more than one tiger, must be integrated by the dreamer — "I have to let them in" — but, understandably, she is "a bit apprehensive".

This archetypal dream had a more personal sequence, which illustrates the subtle interrelationship between the collective and the personal unconscious.

> There are two men, one of whom wants to use me as a prostitute. I don't really want to, but an unknown woman is there who says that it is O.K.; she often does it, she just thinks about something else.

Portrayed in sexual imagery, this dream describes a personal conflict within the dreamer, and one that is also a central part of our patriarchal culture: the woman allowing herself to be used by a man. In the dream there are two men and two women, suggesting the marriage quaternio, a symbol of psychic wholeness, yet in this case the sexual union would not represent integration, as the woman is being "used". It is appropriate here to refer to Esther Harding's understanding of the meaning of the term "virgin":

---

[19] E. Neumann, *The Great Mother* (Princeton, 1972) p. 183n. In China, while the Dragon represents the masculine, yang energy, the Tiger represents the feminine, yin energy. C.G. Jung *Collected Works Vol. 14 Mysterium Coniunctionis* para 403n.

> The term virgin, when used of the ancient goddesses, clearly has a meaning not of today. It may be used of a woman who has had much sexual experience: it may even be applied to a prostitute...A girl belongs to herself while she is a virgin...she is "one-in-herself".[20]

Rather than belonging to a man, a virgin, with or without sexual experience, belongs to the Goddess, to her own feminine self. Similarly, the image of prostitution in this dream refers to the woman denying her own feminine self for the sake of a man, or the masculine; she does not respect the Goddess within. Significantly, it is an "unknown woman", a shadow figure, who "says it is O.K." and "often does it" without being fully aware of what she is doing, "just thinks about something else". As ever, the shadow acts unconsciously, and here suggest that the figure of the dreamer should do likewise. The shadow almost always tries to limit consciousness.

When discussing the dream, the dreamer wanted to know what to do, and it was suggested that she should just become aware of what she was doing; rather than thinking "about something else" she should become conscious of the part within herself that sacrificed her feminine integrity to the man. A few days later she had a dream in which a tiger came and licked her face! After encountering the Goddess, the dreamer had to respect her own feminine self, the Goddess within her; no more could she prostitute herself. But in being aware of that tendency within her, she was no longer apprehensive of the power of the Goddess: the tiger came and licked her face. In order to integrate this primal power and use it creatively one must become conscious of the shadow, for the undifferentiated energy of the unconscious is only dark and frightening when it manifests through the shadow.

I find that this series of dreams offers a profound insight into the relationship between the archetypes and the shadow. Furthermore, while our culture conditions us to think that results are only achieved through "doing something", the final dream shows the effectiveness of just becoming aware. Interestingly, the desire to "do something" is a masculine drive, while inner realization is the result of a feminine approach, one which echoes the Way of the Tao: "Work without doing" [21]

---

[20] M. Esther Harding *Woman's Mysteries* (London 1982) p. 103

[21] Lao Tzu *Tao Te Ching* trans. Gia-Fu Feng and Jane English, (Aldershot 1973) Chapter 63.

In the depths of the unconscious lies the serpent: cold-blooded, it symbolizes the deepest layers of the psyche and, together with the dragon, it is also a symbol for the primordial power of the whole psyche. At some stage on the Path, this great snake must be encountered, for only then can the individual fully transmute the energies of the unconscious. In the following extract from a longer dream, the dreamer is shown by a teacher figure how such a serpent can be approached:

> I visited a swami who had a building of two circular structures on different levels. I followed him to the upper level, where there were a number of his male disciples around a pool. The swami went into the water, and in the water was his beloved serpent. I was kind of merged with the swami, was in him in the water, and I was quite frightened by this huge snake, but he wasn't. He told me that the snake was his great friend because he had surrendered to the snake and it didn't kill him because he was surrendered to it. The snake was his friend because he had accepted it.

This serpent, which inhabited and was contained in the pool, or psyche of the swami, was his friend "because he accepted it". One of the simplest and most fundamental principles of the *Opus* is that through being accepted, "negative" aspects of the unconscious are transformed and integrated. However, this dream offers a spiritual perspective on this process. The dreamer encounters this serpent through being "merged" with the teacher figure. "Merging with the Teacher", *Fana fi Shaikh*, is central to the Sufi Path. It is through first merging with the Teacher, "a complete self annihilation in the Master",[22] that the disciple eventually merges with God, *Fana fi Allah*. In this dream, the dreamer is not fully merged, because, unlike the swami, he "was quite frightened". But this important process has begun.

The serpent did not kill the swami "because he surrendered to it", and this offers an insight into the spiritual implications of surrender. For if one is fully surrendered, one has already died, and therefore cannot be killed:

> When you die of surrender, only then you will live forever,
> If you are put to death through surrender,
> There is no such thing as death for you,

---

[22] Irina Tweedie, op. cit. p. 95.

For you have died already.[23]

The essence of any spiritual path is to learn to surrender, to learn to fully accept whatever is given, given by the Teacher, given by life, which is the greatest Guru, given by God. In a recent television interview, Mother Theresa described what this really means:

> Everyday we have to say yes — total surrender. To be where He wants you to be. If He puts you in the street, if everything is taken from you, when suddenly you find yourself in the street, to accept to be in that street at *that* moment. Not to move, not for you to put yourself in the street, but to accept to be put there. This is quite different. To accept if God wants you to be in a palace, well then to accept to be in the palace so long as you are not choosing to be in the palace. This is the difference in total surrender. To accept what he gives and to give whatever He takes with a big smile. This is the surrender to God. To accept to be cut to pieces and yet every bit to belong only to Him. This is the surrender. To accept all the people that come, the work that you happen to do. To *accept*. And to give whatever it takes; it takes your good name, it takes your health, it takes...yes, you are free then.

To surrender, to accept "the work that you happen to do", to accept the serpent in the depths, this is the Way of the Sufi.

To be constantly surrendered to God, to be His slave and to long for nothing but union with Him, this is the goal of the Sufi. In this final dream, the dreamer stands alone at the altar rail, bound hand and foot:

> I am going to get married, a proper marriage. I am dressed in white and everything is beautiful and fine as one would imagine it. The only thing is that there is no bridegroom. I am walking on my own down the aisle and I see that my whole family and background is sitting in the church pretending that it is a normal wedding taking place. Then I come to the altar and the priest is waiting for me. A little ceremony takes place, the exchange of rings, but the priest puts one ring around both wrists and one around both ankles, then he leans me against the cross and I am faced towards the aisle and then they (my family, etc.) all leave, because they cannot take the situation of me being there like that.

---

[23] ibid. pp. 158-9.

This was dreamt three times by the dreamer, a woman, and according to an esoteric tradition, if something is told three times it must be true.[24]

The dream images the mystical marriage, for the invisible bridegroom is the Beloved, and it is, indeed, a "proper marriage". But in the ceremony, the ring which is a token of this marriage, binds the bride as a slave, "one ring around both wrists, and one around both ankles". In the dream of the woman "walking on a tightrope", "a gold ring around my left foot" imaged the dreamer as a slave of God, but here at the altar the rings more explicitly portray the slavery of the dreamer, who can no longer move of her own free will. Bound hand and foot, she is then leant against the cross, symbolizing the crucifixion that will take her to God. On the cross, the ego will die; this is the arena for those committed to the Path. And at this point the family and background of the dreamer "all leave, because they cannot take the situation of me being there like that", for they represent the conditioning and worldly ties of the dreamer, which must fall away in order to leave the soul free to go to God. But significantly, it is they who leave the dreamer once she is married and on the cross, for on the Sufi Path it is the aspiration and commitment of the disciple that effects the process of psychological change. Just as the simple meditation of the heart activates the psyche and catalyzes the process of alchemical transformation, so too, in the very process of surrender do the worldly attachments, both physical and psychological, fall away, leaving an empty cup waiting to be filled with the wine of the Beloved.

Llewellyn Vaughn-Lee was born in 1953 and has followed the Naqshbandi Sufi Path since he was 19. An English literature teacher by profession, his study of Jungian Psychology was the result of a dream in 1982 in which he was told to read the works of Jung. He has recently completed a Ph.D. dissertation on Archetypal Psychology and Shakespeare.

---

[24] Similarly, if a question is asked three times it must be answered, as in the Katha Upanishad, when the boy Nachiketas meets the Spirit of Death, and asks to be taught the truth about death.

The Transcendent Function And Psychotherapy — A Sufi Perspective

By Don Weiner

Jung described the psychological transcendent function as arising from the union of conscious and unconscious contents. Therapy is a process of overcoming the separation between the conscious and the unconscious, and as a result arriving at a new attitude. Dreams, spontaneous fantasies, and directed fantasies are a very important source of materials to bring about the transcendent function.

From the Sufi vantage point, spiritual growth results from awakening from a limited, individual perspective to discover the richness of all the levels of one's being. Techniques are incorporated to unfold in four directions of consciousness: the cosmic dimension, turning within, the transcendental dimension, and awakening in life. The cosmic dimension is associated with expansion of consciousness, a sense of being part of all things. Turning within involves withdrawing one's consciousness from the environment and discovering an inner space, while still maintaining a connection with all beings from within. The transcendental dimension is also known as *samadhi*, or awakening beyond life. In this condition, all sense of duality is transcended to experience a state of unity. Awakening in life incorporates creativity and manifestation of one's divine inheritance.

As a psychologist, I have found many of the methods of spiritual development in the Sufi teachings to be very beneficial in the process of psychotherapy. These techniques seem to foster what Jung calls the transcendent function, as they help the patient to achieve a sense of integration and discovery of many aspects of him/herself which were previously unconscious. This paper will describe approaches I have found helpful in treating patients with a variety of psychological disorders.

A faulty self-image underlies many types of psychological problems. The patient may either identify with his/her symptoms, or with a limited sense of self which results in the pattern of symptoms. A change of consciousness can lead to a change in self-image and greater

147

psychological health. Such a change in identity may be brought about by working with one or more of the four directions of consciousness described previously. In addition, the Sufi approach deals with a purpose oriented model of therapy rather than a model based upon causality. On the spiritual path and in life, people go through different *makam* or stations, and in each station different qualities seek to manifest. A problem may be viewed as an opportunity to develop a particular quality that is trying to come through. The solution is not necessarily to make the symptoms of the patient disappear, but to use them as an opportunity for unfoldment.

Psychosomatic symptoms may be recognized as a signal that the patient needs to make a change in his/her life. If the patient can recognize the message the symptom is trying to convey (such as learning assertiveness, expressing anger, achieving balance), then the symptom need not continue to manifest so frequently. Techniques such as visualization may be very effective. I have found that by having the patient describe a psychosomatic symptom in a variety of dimensions, such as size, shape, location, texture, temperature, motion, density, and color, and then systematically altering each dimension, that many symptoms can be cleared up in a very short time. I usually ask the patient to intensify slightly the problem at first. (Everyone feels they can experience more of the symptom.) Once that is accomplished, then the patient has confidence they can influence their symptoms in a positive way as well. For example, a headache may be described as rough, heavy, hot, pulsing, and red. I ask the patient first to visualize the area of the headache as becoming smooth, then lighter, then cooler, then still, and then to use the breath to shift the color to orange, to green, and to blue. Finally, I have the patient visualize dispersing the remaining discomfort throughout the body and with the breath discharging energy that is not beneficial. This technique enables the patient to shift from seeing the symptom as a foreign problem to be eliminated to seeing the symptom as a communication from the unconscious which seeks to establish a healthier state of being. Patients who use this method to eliminate a symptom when it occurs usually quickly discover that if they ignore the purpose behind the symptom, e.g., dealing more appropriately with an interpersonal problem, that the symptom will quickly return.

In working with a problem such as hypertension, the patient may need to learn to change his/her time sense. The type-A personality is often associated with high blood pressure, and such a person continually feels a time pressure. Meditation techniques to focus on the present, as well as breathing exercises and guided imagery can be very beneficial. I have worked with some patients outdoors and had them walk very slowly in nature, observing very carefully their surroundings as they do so. This is extremely difficult for type-A individuals, but with practice, a dramatic shift in consciousness often occurs. The person begins to feel a relationship with their surroundings, rather than feeling a sense of separation and isolation. The patient may then be ready to work with imagery and the breath. After teaching a form of relaxation such as progressive muscle relaxation training, I may have the patient visualize nature images such as a tree and to breathe holding the image of the tree. The breath becomes much calmer and more regular. Other images may include the sky, the ocean, a mountain, or a flower.

The Sufi purification breaths of the four elements may also be very helpful with psychosomatic problems. In the earth purification breath, the patient inhales and exhales through the nose. While inhaling he/she imagines drawing upwards into the body magnetism from the earth, replenishing the magnetic field of the body. While exhaling, the image is discharging energy from the body and the magnetic field which has gotten distorted. This breath practice seems to help the patient restore a sense of balance between the inner and outer dimensions of being.

In the water purification breath, the patient inhales through the nose and draws awareness upwards above the head, imagining celestial light. The patient exhales through the mouth and imagines bathing the body with light. This breath practice is very helpful in depressed patients or patients with guilt or shame.

In the fire purification breath, the patient inhales through the mouth and draws awareness into the solar plexus, feeling heat. The breath is drawn upwards to the heart center and the patient exhales through the nose, transmuting heat into light, and suffering into joy. This breath practice is helpful in patients dealing with intense anger or needing to develop the will and balance it with the emotions.

The air purification breath involves exhaling through the mouth and imaging dispersing into space, and then inhaling through the mouth and contemplating spaciousness in one's being. This breath practice is helpful in patients who are introverted and withdrawn, or those who are overly identified with just the physical aspect of their being.

As in the case of psychosomatic disorders, in working with depressed patients it is important to teach them to learn not to fight their symptoms, but rather to seek to understand the message the symptoms are seeking to convey. Depression may be an indication of a need for a change in a patient's job, relationship, or on a deeper level, a change in one's sense of purpose in life. I have found imagery techniques of having the patient expand consciousness into space to be very helpful. Practices involving visualizing light and landscapes of light are also very useful. While such practices are not a cure for the depression, they give the patient an indication that they can get better and that the depression need not be permanent.

The Buddhist *sattipatana* and *jhanas* meditations are also very helpful in working with depressed patients. These practices enable the patient to learn to shift the sense of consciousness beyond that of identifying with a limited sense of identity. The patient discovers a feeling of connection with other people and with all of life as a remedy to the sense of constriction and isolation which may accompany depression. The patient may feel for the first time an experience of harmony with the forces of life rather than a continual struggle to function in the world. Once this is accomplished, then the patient may utilize practices involving awakening in life. The patient may be encouraged to visualize the way he/she would like to feel — physically, mentally, emotionally, and spiritually. At first these images of an ideal self may seem blurry and unreal, but with practice, the patient learns to establish a clear sense of healthy identity which can be manifested. The patient can then begin to act in situations as if these goals were already realized, and by doing so, the patient develops confidence in a newly emerging and healthier ways of being. In retrospect the patient may realize that without having experienced the depression, he/she may have stayed stuck in an unfulfilling way of life, with a narrow range of experience.

In working with patients with chronic pain, in addition to the techniques described in the section on psychosomatic disorders, transcendent meditation techniques may be very helpful to help the patient obtain relief from pain. The Sufis utilize a variety of techniques to achieve *samadhi* or awakening beyond life. These usually begin with deep relaxation and then releasing identification with one's thoughts, emotions, and personality. One may attune to different currents of energy in the body, such as magnetism, life energy, and pure spirit, and surrender to the forces of life. The breakthrough comes when one releases the efforts of the will to achieve *samadhi* . Following the *samadhi* meditation different types of imagery may be utilized to help mobilize the patient's own internal healing resources. I often have the patient go into a state of deep relaxation and then imagine descending a flight of stairs. At the bottom of the stairs, the patient is instructed to go to the end of a passageway and open a door to a very special room. I instruct the patient that he/she will be able to remain very deeply relaxed but will also be able to communicate his/her experience and answer questions. In the room the patient is instructed that every object has the potential to offer healing or guidance. For example if the patient describes a chair in the room, the instructions are to sit in the chair and either put forth a request for healing or general information, or for an answer to a specific question. The patient almost always experiences exactly what he/she needs to receive. This seems to be an effective way to help the patient access his/her own intuition as well as inner healing resources.

Another visualization which is often helpful in patients with illnesses or chronic pain is to have them visualize a single cell in their body, and the relationship of that cell with the other cells. The meditation continues with imagery to experience the harmony and rhythms of the different organs in the body, systems of the body, and eventually the relationship between the individual and the cosmos.

Visualizations are also very helpful in working with negative emotions. One Sufi practice is the heart purification exercise. This involves imagining the heart center as a sphere with a mirror coating. The coating has become tarnished over the years with the residue of unresolved emotions such as anger, guilt, fear, resentment, jealousy, etc. The patient is instructed to imagine breathing in white light through the nostrils and taking the light to the heart center, using the light to gently remove the tarnish and send the tarnish out with the breath. In this way the patient can begin to release emotions he/she is ready to resolve. The patient is instructed that he/she may re-experience old emotions during the exercise, but rather than the usual tendency to close the heart when these emotions arise, the patient is to keep the heart center open. A similar visualization involves the patient imagining cords extending from different places on the body to people or situations in which there is some unresolved emotion. The patient visualizes cutting the cords with a crystal and becoming free from a former emotional bind. When a cord is cut, the patient visualizes light emanating from the point the cord was attached to.

There are a number of visualizations used by the Sufis known as landscapes of the soul. These are used to help an individual develop particular qualities which are latent. To help a person develop guidance, he/she may imagine steering a boat at sea on a foggy night, just barely being able to see a light from a lighthouse on the horizon.

The patient steers toward the lighthouse and safe harbor, overcoming obstacles such as fog, wind, doubt, and fear. This practice is helpful with a person who lacks a sense of direction in his/her life.

To help an individual access the bounty of qualities which may be latent in their personality, the patient may visualize a stream of water flowing from left to right, and feel that qualities are being released in his/her being as the stream flows. In the case where an individual lacks vitality, he/she may imagine standing beneath a waterfall and being replenished with life energy.

For a person who feels defiled by a traumatic experience such as rape, visualizing a landscape of ice and snow and seeing s stream of pure water flowing from the melting snow at the top of a mountain may help to restore a sense of purity and sacredness. The Sufis use the metaphor of the inner self as a mirror which can never be sullied; the problem is that the individual identifies with the reflection in the mirror. Imagery can help the patient experience the deepest aspect of his/her being and restore a sense of wholeness.

Visualization may also be very effective with children. I have found that having a child imagine watching a television set and putting on different channels to help them with different problems is very effective. The child can imagine seeing a special friend on different channels that he/she can call on for help.

For both children and adults, music is very helpful in visualizations. Music helps the patient achieve a state of relaxation and to establish a particular attunement depending on the type of imagery. Music with sounds of water and birds is helpful in nature visualizations. "Space music" is helpful in cosmic meditations. Sacred music such as Gregorian Chants or Buddhist or Hindu Chants can be very helpful, depending on the beliefs of the patient.

In the case where a patient feels he/she is totally lacking in a particular quality which is needed to deal with a problem, then the patient can be asked to think of a person who embodies that quality. The patient is asked to imagine how that person would handle the problem. Later the patient is encouraged to visualize how he/she would deal with the problem if he/she possessed the quality of the other person. Eventually the patient discovers his/her own ability to express a quality which was previously thought to be absent. A related meditation which may be helpful is known as the ideal master meditation. The patient is asked to visualize a remarkable being of great strength, compassion, insight, magnetism, power, truth, etc. The patient feels all of these qualities very strongly emanating from the master and visualizes incorporating these qualities into his/her own being. Finally the patient sees that the ideal master is none other than his/her real self.

Jung recognized the importance of the therapist recognizing the potentialities which he/she seeks to make conscious in the patient through the transcendent process. The Sufis also share this perspective, and teach that by a guide (or therapist) perceiving that which transpires behind that which appears, that this insight helps to awaken latent qualities in the patient. The therapist can only take the patient to the level of realization which the therapist has attained. The techniques described in this paper can only be effective to the degree the therapist has worked with them and made them a reality in his/her own life.

In my psychotherapy practice with patients techniques are useful tools towards helping patients unfold on all levels of their being. Beyond techniques, however, the most important issue is the ability to experience a deep connection with my patients beyond the words that are said and beyond the content of the sessions. If a very deep connection can be established with a patient, then very profound changes can take place in the patient, and these changes are much less dependent upon the methods utilized than upon the therapeutic relationship and atmosphere of attunement and healing. I have found that my growth on the spiritual path has greatly enriched my work as a psychologist, and what I learn from sharing the joy and suffering of my patients has contributed to my unfoldment. I used to think of psychology and spirituality as distinct and separate entities, but over the years I have realized that this dichotomy was an illusion. The teachings of Jung are very much in harmony with the Sufi teachings, and both have much to offer to the field of psychology.

The Arab: A Story In The Sufi Style

By J. Marvin Spiegelman

Introduction

The following tale, modelled in the Sufi style of adventure, moral and transformation, is taken from the author's book, *The Tree: Tales in Psychomythology*. In that book, ten different spiritual paths are revealed, in the form of ten tales by as many individuals. Buddhists, Christians, Jews, Taoists, Hindus, Atheists, Pagans, Pantheists, Gnostics are represented, as well as the one herein offered, that of a Muslim telling his own tale in Sufi fashion. At the outset, our hero addresses himself to the initial teller of tales, a Knight who has told of his own transformation in Gnostic terms. Our Sufi at first tries to enlighten the Knight and then proceeds to his own story of personal transformation.

The author hopes that his tale is true to the genre and that his attempt at verisimilitude will be greeted as an indication of honor and respect from one outside that tradition but appreciating it immensely.

I

I am an Arab. Neither Christian nor Jew, nor any mixture, but simply an Arab. I am one of the tribe of Ishmael and Esau, blessed be him who was deceived and betrayed. Unlike my friend, the Knight, my encounters have been with men, not Gods. That is not entirely true since, as Jews and Christians are aware, God is not realized apart from men, and if you wish to know God, you must know man, and know him in the flesh. I have nothing personally against Jews or Christians — the father of us all is Abraham, after all — though these people have committed many sins against my people. No matter, I am here to tell you a tale and not to engage in religious polemics. I respect you, Sir Knight, in any case, since you, after all, are on the same quest for Allah that we are all on. Enough! To my story.

One there was a brutal blue calf. You must try to visualize this. It should be easy for you to visualize a blue calf, but brutal may be somewhat difficult for you. I will explain in what way he, this calf, was brutal. He was brutal in that he ate grass without regard for anything. Not only did he eat his master's fine field of grass, and thus deprive all the other cattle of their fodder, but he also ate into the neighbor's fields. He did so incessantly, and with a greed and an appetite which was both wonderful and horrible to behold. He was not an especially large calf, and extraordinary in no other way except in his color and his appetite. What was the meaning of this strange event of nature? Why did this calf appear to us? We did not know.

One understood from the outset that this calf was unusual. Not only from his color, but from the fact that he weaned himself from his mother within minutes after he was born. He sucked a bit, licked his mouth, as if to say "That's all right, but I would rather be on my own" and promptly started eating grass. He could hardly stand on his wobbly little legs, but grass he could eat aplenty.

At first we were all amused by this funny little calf. We called all the people, from far and wide, to see our strange little animal. We petted him, and encouraged him, to which he responded not at all. After a time, however, the calf was no longer amusing. Rather, he became too much for his master. The master tried all sorts of ways to restrain him. He tied him up — but the calf broke loose. He confined him to a fenced-in place — but the calf somehow managed to dig a tunnel overnight. Now we knew that we were dealing not only with an unusual animal, but that, indeed, he was a monster.

A meeting was called of all the neighbors, for this is what Arabs sometimes do, in the face of a community problem. Each neighbor had a different idea of what to do with the calf. Some were for killing him at once, since he was such a menace to all. Others were horrified by this idea, since it seemed cruel. Still others thought that the calf was a special creation of the Almighty and had, therefore, to be humored and respected, much as one behaved, in the ancient days, with epileptics. Still others tried to minimize the problem and played the game of hoping it would all go away. The meetings were inconclusive, so all went out to smoke hashish.

The calf went right on eating. In their hashish dreams, some of the people wondered what would happen when this monstrous calf would grow up and become a bull — as if the extent of his destruction were not enough already — but they seemed strangely impotent to do anything about it. As for myself, I had the suspicion that the people really wanted the calf to continue his greediness, and that they had an inkling of what was to come. Since I did not live there myself, and since my view is, as far as possible, not to interfere in Allah's wondrous ways, I held my tongue and enjoyed my hashish with the rest.

A curious thing happened. When the members of the community seemed to abandon any effort to restrain this peculiar animal, when they simply left the matter to God, the calf, for the first time, pricked up his ears and seemed to notice them. Until that time, our precious calf had a marvelous indifference to all those around him. You will recall that he soon abandoned his mother's teat and showed every sign of total disinterest in everything except grass. Now, however, he came to where the group of neighbors were and looked at them. He was puzzled by their lack of interest in him — or so it seemed to me — and did not know what to do.

My neighborly friends quickly noticed this despite their hashish dreams, and slyly winked at one another. They puffed and waited. The calf peered at them for a long time. He then, of his own accord, leaped back into the fenced-in area that had been provided for him earlier.

We all thought: Allah has spoken. Do you need an interpretation of this event, Sir Knight? I trust that you do not. In any case, I am not going to provide it for I cannot. When you have heard me through, you will surely grasp what I am trying to say, beyond the words. I will go on, now, to another tale.

II

You will have grasped, Sir Knight, that one message of my tale is not to interfere in God's wondrous ways. Nature will restrain itself. That, no doubt, is a very bitter medicine for you to swallow, but listen further.

Once there was a marvelous fairy queen who lived alone in the heart of a forest. She was by no means a Sleeping Beauty, since she was wide awake. She was, indeed, beautiful beyond man's belief, but she had seen so much of the worlds, both natural and supernatural, that she retired to her fairy glen to be alone and have none of it. Many were the knights who came to woo her, but none could reach her. She was surrounded by nettles and by plants with gummy substances, the penetration of which caused a person to be hopelessly caught and entwined beyond the possibility of extrication. The great circle of these plants became the final resting place for many a warrior and knight. Their bare bones were ample warning for would-be conquerors.

One day, a Knight such as yourself came along, who was particularly pure in heart. Most of the other knights who dared to seek out the fairy queen came in the spirit of conquest, lust, fame, and other such worldly desires. This young Knight, however, was different. He was, indeed, like yourself, on a quest for the Almighty. He had, of course, a full measure of the generality of human vices, but was redeemed only by this one virtue.

Our young Knight journeyed to the glen of the fairy queen on the command of an Angel, and did not even know why he was so ordered. Now this, of course, was known to the fairy queen and, though her heart had been hardened by her experience of men's willfulness and greed, she took pity on the young Knight. She would certainly not yield to him, nor even answer his questions, but when she saw him struggling in the morass of nettles, gum, and bones of other knights, she mercifully made a path for him. The Knight lurched forward and fell panting and in pain at her feet.

After freeing him, the fairy queen promptly returned to her resting place and gave no other thought to the intruder.

The young Knight recovered from his breathlessness and the pain of his struggle and looked at the fairy queen. The queen ignored him. The young Knight spoke:

"Madam, I do not know why I have been sent here. As you probably know — for such has been my experience on each of my adventures — I have been sent here by an Angel, and I believe that I am supposed to learn something from you."

"Knight," responded the fairy queen, "you are very boring indeed. I took pity on you because you were pure in heart, and on a quest. Do you not see that I have had enough of the world, both natural and supernatural, and that whatever your desire may be it is of no interest to me? Go and tell your Angel that I am bored with him, too!"

Our poor young Knight was crestfallen. This was the worst affront possible. To be thought of as aggressive, deep, lofty, apart from other men — all of this was not painful to him. To be thought of, even, as a fool, provided it was the "fool of God", also was quite acceptable to him. To be called a bore, however, was the deepest wound of all, and he could do nothing except sit down and look sheepish.

Then he started to laugh. He began to laugh and laugh, until his sides ached and belly hurt. "Yes," he thought, "I am indeed a bore! What a boring fellow am I! I come to a fairy queen only because the Angel tells me to. I do not do it on my own accord, or out of my own desire. I do not really take any responsibility in all this, and so I am only a clean-cut, pure sort of thing, mother's little knight, perhaps." He laughed and laughed. "Yes," he continued, and now aloud, "those poor fellows with their bones bleaching in the sun, those bags of bones have more honor than I! They, at least, knew what they were after, knew what desire they had. Yes, madam, I beg your pardon, I am indeed a bore, and will now go back home and tend my garden."

With that, our Knight turned on his heels and started to walk back out of the sacred circle. The fairy queen got red as a beet and screamed at the Knight.

"You are not only boring, you are also exasperating! Why, you, you..." She spluttered in her rage, and the Knight was halted in his tracks. With a wave of her hand, the Knight was again embroiled in the nettles and gum, this time battling to get out.

In the midst of his struggle, he shook his head at the imponderability of women, both natural and supernatural, and decided that there was no purpose in continuing. He would do better to surrender and die as these others had died, leaving his bones as warning for his brother knights who might come in the future.

But the fairy queen, with her unpredictable nature, was not going to let him die so easily. Once again she parted the ways for him. Was she becoming aware of her own desire for the Knight? The Knight fell panting to the ground again. Now he looked up at the fairy queen with puzzlement in his face, and asked, imploringly, "Madam, what do you want of me? I have left you in peace, am willing to die like a dog and let my bones bleach in the sun, and you do not let me!"

The fairy queen fumed and spluttered. She was about to encompass him once again in the nettles and gum, but she stopped and laughed instead. Now she laughed as the Knight had laughed — deeply, heartily, and with chagrin at herself.

"Knight," she said, "I beg your pardon. I see that whatever I do to you is wrong. I must confess that I did not know that I desired you myself. It is ever so much more noble to retreat from the world, both natural and supernatural, and be sought after, than to acknowledge that one is desirous oneself. Yes, I see that you have won because you did, indeed, know what you wanted, to serve God. I was furious because you did not want me, whereas I did not know that I wanted you."

The Knight rubbed his wounds and shook his head. "Madam, I no longer know what I want, nor do I know what God wants, and I really do not much care what you want. I am beginning to think that the Buddhists are perhaps right. Desire and wanting is the ground of ignorance, for God and man!" Thus speaking, the Knight fell to his knees and hit the ground with his fists.

Now the fairy queen grew puzzled. She looked at the Knight in hurt and anger, and then started to cry. The Knight was startled by her tears, and came over to her. "Madam," he said, "why are you weeping? I did not intend to hurt you."

"You did not hurt me, you fool!...Yes, you did. I told you I wanted you, and you ignored me. Do you not know that is the greatest sin against a woman, human or divine!" With that she arose and strode away.

The Knight mused to himself: "Yes, that is how a woman is — no, not a woman, a woman would be more human — that is how a goddess or fairy queen or sprite is. She sits there unmindful of the death and suffering of hundreds of men who know exactly what they want — her — and gets all aflutter if her needs are not subtly and delicately apprehended at once. Well, I am still alive, and very doubtful indeed whether I want her or not. She can just sit there until she gets more human!"

The Knight rubbed his wounds, and bolstered his pride. The fairy queen sat to one side, more peevish than anything else. They sat thus apart for a very long time. Then, at the same moment, they looked up at each other, smiled, and embraced.

III

Thus far, Sir Knight, my tale has been for you, to edify you in ways that might be helpful to you, since you are something of a moralist.

Before I tell of my experiences, however, I must first say something about myself. I am said to be a handsome man, and I believe it, though such things are, as everyone knows, in the eye of the beholder. I am also said to be an honorable man, though in a way quite different from the Knight. I am honorable in love. That is it. My morals are quite different from Sir Knight, and I have no wrathful Eye of God to placate at every turn. One might say that I serve a Goddess of Love — though I think of it in no such grand or literal terms, since that would be to offend Allah, who will brook no polytheism. I know only that in serving love, I am also serving the Almighty, for that is my deepest nature and Allah put me here, I believe, to be myself and no other.

When I was a young man, I lived in a city far from here. I was a studious and serious fellow, much involved with my books and my plans were to become either a physician or mathematician. My family was illustrious in both realms and I wanted to follow my ancestral path. I was quiet and reflective, but not withdrawn from life. I enjoyed my friends and the luxurious life made possible by the wealth of my family, but my studies came first. Nor was I aggressive. My body was strong so that few cared to contend with me, but neither did I need to prove myself or seek out the competitive duels and combats of my friends. This was all as it should be — since it was understood that I would be a scholar or healer and no one expects such a person to be violent, even in Arab lands. The reason that I dwell on this fact will be apparent later on.

My life proceeded peacefully and amicably. I was betrothed to a worthy woman of a family of as high a standing as my own and we were pleased with each other. The wedding was to take place at the conclusion of my studies, which was only a few months away and I was in good spirits.

One day, however, as I was looking over the pages of an old volume at a bookstall in the street, I chanced to look up and caught a glimpse of the most beautiful dark eyes that I had ever seen. The girl was veiled and covered from head to foot, except for her eyes. When I saw them, my heart was stricken. To say that an arrow pierced my heart would be foolish. Say only, and more accurately, that I was possessed. I knew that I had to see that girl again, to gaze at her, to have her.

She vanished along the street, in the company of another woman. I hurried after them, but could find them nowhere. Shaken to my foundations, I knew that I could not survive unless I saw that girl again. Studies, marriage, career, all vanished as if they were only an illusion. I searched for her everywhere and made inquiries. It was impossible, of course, because how can one describe an identity from eyes alone? Yet the beauty in these eyes were enough to change the course of a life.

That evening I wandered, disconsolate, into the desert. A yellow crescent moon glowed in the sky as if it had an inner source of light, not reflecting the golden sun setting proudly at the horizon. I sat down on a rock and held my head in my hands. What was I to do? I knew that my life could not continue without that unknown girl, who was already in my thoughts as my beloved. The evening changed into night and I felt chilled. I gathered my cloak around me and started to walk. I walked aimlessly until I saw, in the distance, the red light of a campfire.

Coming close to the fire, I observed a wizened old woman, calmly cooking her supper. She glanced at me quickly and returned to her task. Unwilling or unable to utter a word, I sat down by her fire and warmed myself. We sat silently until the woman offered me a soup which I accepted gratefully to thaw my frozen bones and benumbed heart.

The woman spoke: "I see a young man lost in love. I see him finding his beloved and, in the finding, losing himself. I see heights of ecstasy and bottomless pits of pain." She expressed what I already knew, somewhere deep inside myself, and accepted. Such was the will of

Allah, and such was to be my fate. A peace overcame me. I crossed her palm with silver and, without a word, walked back to the city.

When I returned to the city, I was still calm, though feeling a growing excitement at the expected re-encounter with my beloved. I knew that I would find her, and that my life would be changed. I also knew that it was the will of Allah. I let myself be guided by my steps and found my way back to the bookstall where I had first glimpsed her.

It was night, and the stall was closed, but life was continuing in the streets. The muezzin's chant of the evening prayer had ended and the people were swarming about. Among them all, just across the cobbled street, stood the girl, staring intently at me. I caught my breath, felt my knees quiver as our eyes united in irresistible attraction. I slowly crossed the street.

When I reached her, I put my arms on her shoulders and looked deeply into those eyes which openly received me and drew me in. My soul plunged into their depths as into an unknown abyss where pain and ecstasy are as one. We said not a word to each other, for what was there to say?

I could not embrace her, since this was not proper in my city, nor could I spirit her away, since her companion was close by. After we had gazed at each other for some few seconds of eternity, she slipped me a note and hurried off.

For a long time, I stood transfixed on the spot, savoring the memory and unwilling to leave the trancelike state I was in. At last, I lifted up my hand, holding the note, and held it tightly, though careful not to crush it. I dared not read it at that moment, for its import was too great to be taken in at that unprotected place.

I hurried to my home and my room and only then did I feel free to expose myself to its contents and allow whatever emotion they produced to take hold of me. The words were simple and brief: "I love you. Meet me tomorrow night." What more was there to be said? How many words I had read in books! And these were the most important of my life.

I slept hardly at all that night, but was filled with desire and restlessness. Only a glimpse of the moon, outside my window, calmed me and my agitated heart.

Next day I went through the motions of my life, but lived elsewhere. No one, I am sure, knew of my state, nor did I feel that I was dissembling. I found that one could live in two places at once, though the one seemed more like a dream. But which was the dream and which the reality? It did not matter. Reflections such as these came to me from habit and from the past, but they seemed to matter little in the face of the feelings that I was having. These feelings gave me delight I had never known.

That night I went to the marketplace and waited at the same place, across from the bookstall. A plan had been forming in my mind, but it was clouded by wild hopes and despair. Was it not possible that this light of my life would be my wife? Could I not fit into the fabric of my ancestral pattern this wild and irrational gift from the Almighty? It seemed quite reasonable. My parents were decent and loving people, far from reproving the experience of love. Even my betrothed would be made to understand and would surely be sought after by hosts of promising young men of the city. Yet something in me knew that this was all wish and illusion. The soothsayress had spoken the truth, though I knew not why. A sadness overcame me.

A moment later the sadness was lifted, for there, before me, was my beloved, veiled like a clouded moon, but radiant with the soft light that shines from her on a darkened night. We met, took hands, and walked out of the city into the desert. Without a word, we walked to a nearby oasis and sat down by its waters. The light of the same moon which was like my beloved caused everything to appear soft and textured, while the gentle wind made the palm fronds tremble just so slightly.

We reached out our arms and held shoulders, as if each was trying to embrace, grasp, comprehend, and adore the other at the same moment. I dared not lift the veil just yet, since I was conflictually filled with both longing to do so and dread. Instead, I let my hands gently fall from her shoulders and follow the outline of her body down the sides. The softness and hardness blended into a graceful line which went through my fingers, up into my arms and radiated through me until I trembled just as the palm fronds did.

My hands had their own life, and paused in their journey at her waist. For an instant, I hesitated, and was gripped with passion. I pulled her to me with force and reached behind her to press her to me. But the force was unnecessary, since she melted into me of her own will — or was it a will higher than both of us? Our bodies met as if two broken pieces of a bowl were re-united into one vessel where only the seam could be seen.

We held each other so for a long time. The warmth of her body and her love calmed my agitated desire and made me human again. At last, I gently lifted her veil and kissed her deeply on the mouth, not even needing to gaze at the face for its true being was already known to me in an utterly imageless way. Our eyes closed and our souls met in the depths of that kiss — lips touching in that seamed and gentle way of the matching shards of a cup. Moments later our mouths opened and our tongues sought the hidden and moist crevices of the other. Now we were in total embrace, each searching and grasping the other in gentleness and violence, all at once.

It was enough. As if at a signal, we separated and sat down to gaze at each other. Need I say that she was lovely? Her face matched her eyes, with full and sensuous lips and rounded cheeks and curves and lines of endless interest and joy. I longed to follow all the lines therein, and yielded to my longing. She smiled as I did so, until, when I had marked out the glowing form to my contentment, I held her head in my hands and drew her towards me for our second kiss. This one was quick and playful and settling, as if to say, "and that is that, is that!"

We looked at each other and laughed. The merriness of her eyes and of her face delighted me, for with the depth and intensity that I had seen before, it was almost too much to add merriness and joy. Thus it was that the Almighty had sent her to me.

We had yet to speak a word, and my first ones were, "I love you." To these, she simply nodded and blew me a kiss. Words were...what were they? Nuisances, meaningless addenda? Yes. Most of all, they were irrelevant. I did not know her name, her ancestry, her place, her station in life — all of which would be important in the world from which I came — and did not care. No, that is not true. I cared, but it seemed a violation to even ask them. For her part, she said nothing and asked nothing. She simply looked at me, sometimes held out her hand, to touch or be touched and she seemed content that we were together among the palms and by the water.

It grew late, and I said, "We must go."

"Tomorrow?" she asked.

"Tomorrow," I answered. We walked, hand in hand, back to the city, under the clouded light of the moon, and with a touch of the finger, parted where we had met.

Once home, I could reflect a little. Why were we both unable to speak? Did she, too, have this nameless knowledge of the soothsayress that our love was destined to be tragic? I tried to wipe this knowledge out of my mind. Tomorrow, I thought, we must talk and plan, for there is joy in life, and the doom-laden messages of soothsayers are often wrong. So comforted, I fell asleep.

When I awakened, I felt as if I had a dream, but could not capture it. What was it? What came to my mind was the memory of the soothsayress' words: "I see him finding his beloved and, in the finding, losing himself. I see heights of ecstasy and bottomless pits of pain." Were these in a dream? I did not think so, but suddenly I realized that she said not a word about tragedy, or tragic endings. Losing oneself in the beloved could also mean to find oneself, could it not? Ecstasy and pain are not, necessarily, tragic. I felt comforted, but a small corner of dread persisted. I had fantasies of violence, but from an unnamed source. These, too, I wiped away and lightheartedly went about my day's duties.

That night, we met again and all dread was banished from my thoughts. We ran quickly into the desert, though it was darker now, with hardly any moon at all. We found our way to the oasis and embraced eagerly. I was wild with desire and she seemed to be the same. I clumsily removed her clothes and trembled in my eagerness, hardly aware of the new restraint she was now showing. I felt it as a maidenish encouragement and it made me even wilder in my desire. I grabbed and I lunged and I took her, as some wild man might.

Then it was over. I was cold and hard, and did not know myself. Then I heard her crying, and looked into her eyes. The light had gone out of them, and now there was only agony. I could not look at her. I turned and ran. I ran, deep into the desert, deep into the darkness, as a hyena would run into a cave; as if knowing his instinctive demonism, hiding this from the world and, if he could, from himself.

I ran until I was exhausted and fell in a heap. First, all was confusion, despair, and agony. Exhaustion was blended with self-hatred and despair with confusion. When I recovered my breath, I ran again. I ran as if the only thing that would calm the violence directed at myself was running. Again exhaustion, again collapse. I must have run most of the night until, at last, I slept.

When I awakened, I was calm and not at all agitated. With clarity, I saw what I was: a man without love. In the recesses of my soul lurked a loveless creature, cold and hard and with a selfish brutality that was beyond my comprehension. I understood why I had refrained from the competitive games and duels. It was not because I was a gentle man, or of the scholarly type, but because I was loveless and not to be trusted. I understood my dread, and regretted my suppression of it. I understood, too, that I knew nothing of myself or of life and that I had to go into the world to find out who I was, or what I was, and find some way to scourge this demon of lovelessness.

I calmly returned to the city, wrote a letter to my beloved explaining what I must do, entrusting it to a friend. I took a few of my possessions, bade goodbye to my parents and my betrothed and left to wander the face of the world. I tried to explain why I must leave, but none understood. But leave, I must, and so I did.

IV

When I left my ancestral home, I knew clearly that I must make my way to the sea. Just as what had emerged in me was the opposite of all that I had thought had resided in my soul, I knew that I must leave all I knew and go to its opposite in the world.

The days of my journey to the sea were long and uneventful. People were kind to me and there were no untoward incidents. The long days of walking also gave me time to reflect upon myself and what had happened. Slowly some perspective came to me and I saw myself more clearly. What had I discovered? That I had a deep capacity for love and its opposite — all at the same time. Before I had met my beloved, I was a quietly contented man, not subject to extremes of any kind. After meeting my beloved, however, I knew I was capable of depths of good and evil. I knew, now, why I had eschewed violence — there was a dangerous and greedy hyena who made his home inside my soul. I was no longer shocked nor guilty about this presence — since this was as much a part of the being that Allah had given me as my love — but knew that something had to be done about it. I concluded that the hyena needed to be fed. If he were fed enough and contented, perhaps he would not be so greedy to devour the good soul upon whom my heart wished to lavish its love. And where should he feed? Of course, where there were other hyenas and jackals and their prey. From stories I had read as a child, I knew that a somewhat civilized jungle existed among soldiers and sailors. My hyena did not want to kill, only to devour, so it was the sailor's life I chose. Hunter-sailor I became, and so harkened back to my ancestors of a dimmer past and the demands of an immediate present.

It was easy for me to find a ship that would have me, for there was a war at that time, and much need of men who would fight or work on those ships which carried goods and men from place to place.

The ship that accepted me was called the "Victory" and its crew readily incarnated the vision that my mind's eye had conjured. I saw their souls as animals, much like my own. First there was the Captain, an old and mangy lion who loftily kept himself apart from all the lesser animals. Then there was the Mate, an arrogant and cruel vulture who viewed us all as underlings to provide him what he needed. His first order to me, when he learned that I had been a student, was to give me the lowliest work on the ship. Perhaps he was right to do so, since I was still arrogant, not fully aware that I was, in truth, an animal like the rest. I did his bidding with the subtle obstructionism that the weak use against the strong.

Then there was the Bosun, a weasel of a man — canny, clever, and self-serving. My fellow sailors included an able and clever tiger, hyenas like myself, and assorted dogs and cats. I resolved to stay close to the tiger, for does not the tiger provide prey which the hyena can devour? When I realized that the enemy of the hyena is the vulture, I was delighted with the rightness of my situation.

So the time went peacefully on our first days at sea. The animals were sharpening their claws with little fights, pacing the deck in their hungers and quietly going about their work, which momentarily distinguished them as men from the animals in their souls. I was easily accepted, once they knew that I did not think myself a lion as a result of my studies, and they heartily laughed when I told them of my animal visions of them all. This endeared them to me, for a man who knows he is an animal is far more to be trusted than one who thinks he is not.

Our first port was in Egypt, and we hungrily went ashore for our food. I attached myself to the tiger, an old and experienced hunter, as did several of the other hyenas and dogs and cats. He led us to a brothel, where a large variety of willing animals, of all colors and races greeted us cordially. There were fat ones and thin ones, tall and short — pigs, cats, and hyenas like myself. My comrades fell to, as soon as the tiger chose his own, a particularly hefty pig, and were joyous. My own hyena, however, refused to eat. Even when cajoled, he declined, so I had to beg pardon and quietly walked down the stairs, to wander in the streets.

Before I had time to reflect upon the perversity of my hyena, and before I had even reached the ground floor, I heard a singing voice which startled me. I turned the corner and walked into a room with a dirt floor and bare, stained walls. The voice belonged to a gaunt Arab man, like myself, who was seated in a stiff chair, strumming an instrument I had never seen. Before him was a gaudily luxurious couch upon which sat a mountainously fat woman. She mounted the couch like a sphinx, arms folded and eyes dreamily inward. Her dress was a bright red, with yellow flowers, and she wore a number of bracelets. Her brown flesh billowed out all around her, but she was majestic in her ampleness. At her feet sat a mouse of a dog, as skinny and bony as she was fat and fleshy.

The Madame — for such she was in this house — motioned me to a chair with the merest blink of an eye. I sat down and listened to the music. The intense young tenor sang of love's pain and joy. I wept with loneliness for my beloved, but the songs soothed my soul, nonetheless.

Thus we sat, and for a long time. I drifted off into timelessness... I was brought back into time by the laughing sounds of the tiger and my friends coming down the stairs. Tiger tapped me on the shoulder — it was time to return to the ship. I bowed my thanks to the Great Madame and her Serenader, which they acknowledged with a nod, and my friends and I were soon walking in the night.

There was good natured teasing of the tastes of my hyena, but my comrades respected my stillness. We returned to the vessel as animals come back to their lairs.

Next day, the tiger and I set out across the desert to see the great Sphinx. We arrived, weary and hot, but were rewarded with a prospect of that eternal statue which spoke to our depths. The Sphinx put no riddles and we asked no questions. All was as it was, and should be. I knew that the perversity of my hyena was so because I did not understand him and what he wanted — no, that was not entirely true. My hyena knew what he wanted, but my soul knew, too, and now the one or the other could triumph. I told the tiger these thoughts and he nodded his head in assent. He then looked at the Great Sphinx and said, "both must be fed to their full."

So ended my first voyage and my second adventure into the meaning of love.

V

"Both must be fed." With this thought of the tiger and myself at the foot of the Sphinx, I spent many a later voyage. I was lucky, indeed, that the "Victory" was destined to make a circumambulation of the globe. From Egypt our course was west and north and south and west again. We journeyed to the Arab lands and to lands of the Vikings. We saw the lands of the dark ones of the south, and the yellow ones, as well. And always I sought to attend to the needs of the soul and the needs of the flesh.

But rarely would they meet. The needs of my soul were met in the temples of religion and the temples of art. Strange and wondrous were the ways that the peoples served their gods, and I knew that they all saw Allah in their own manner. The needs of the flesh were met by the variety of the women I met and had — light, dark, ample, lean. The desires of the flesh were immediate and powerful, those of the soul lasting and more variegated. It seemed that my lusts were satisfied, but in truth they were not. The soul did not restrain the flesh, but would not participate in its satisfaction. So I tried to force the soul into it and then out of it. The former was impossible and the latter very difficult. I broke my Moslem law and drank of the fiery waters. This made me joyous and carefree, but did not drown the pain of my soul.

I tried to surfeit the hyena in every way that I could, sometimes with many women, sometimes in utter abandonment. This led only to vomitus and despair. By now I was indistinguishable from all the other sailor-animals and my tiger friend no longer accompanied me. It was as if he knew that I was become as a tiger myself and now must find my own way. Even the vulture and the lion kept their distance from me as I now became wilder in my attempt to kill the one side or the other in me.

The months went by and my conflict increased. The days and nights at sea, and the blessed needs of work gave me the time for reflection and pause. The days and nights on land found me hungrily seeking my goal.

Finally, exhausted, I came ashore in India. I was refreshed with all the new sights and strange manners. I was entranced by their music and by their dance. I was delighted with the temples and with their art. But so had I been pleased before, in all the other wondrous countries that I had seen. Neither delight nor new sights could satisfy me, however. What was I to do with the animal inside me who would neither be stilled, nor allowed full rein?

In despair of finding a union of body and soul, animal and feeling, I wandered about and found my way to the Temple of Kali, the great many-armed Mother Goddess of the Hindus.

I did not know her story, and was not inclined to inquire too deeply into this polytheistic religion which would be an abomination to my still entrenched monotheism. I knew, in my depths, that my experience of all these other faiths was merely esthetic, and the true religion of my soul was the battle of the animal against love, of soul vs. body.

The Temple of Kali was small, as temples go, but beautiful. It was constructed of myriads of tiles of various colors. Within the holy of holies, I understood that the toe of the Great Goddess was enshrined. It seems that she was dismembered in the heavens, all her parts falling to places where temples were subsequently built. It was not the theology or the story which gripped me. No. There, in the midst of the altar lay a dead and sacrificial goat. His eyes were bulging, and many parts of him were cut away. The pilgrims had taken their holy toll of the animal and went away satisfied.

When I looked at the dead, staring eyes of that goat, I knew something that could not be put into words. I knew only that the goat was myself. I knew that what I had called hyena and tiger, were indeed all that, but here was their grim representative. Ancestral memories were revived, and I remembered with pain the lamented goatskin of Esau and of his deception by Jacob. I remembered our father, Abraham, and of the miraculous animal which took the place of his son. I knew that the goat, this strange goat in a strange temple in a strange land, was that same goat which has plagued the people forever. Here it was, stilled and sacrificed.

I stood long at the altar, eyes magnetized by the eyes of the goat, vaguely aware of the buzzing of flies about his carcass. Soon I became conscious of voices. A little group of musicians and singers were chanting from their holy books, *Mahabarhata* or *Ramayana*. I did not know the words or the story, but was soothed by the hypnotic repetition of the voices. An old wise man, dressed in a simple white cloth, addressed me. He spoke wise words, I know, but I heard nothing. I understood one thing only, the goat was sacrificed, and I could love. A great peace overcame me.

As night fell and the crescent moon rose in the sky, a young man pulled at my sleeve, insistently. I was drawn out of my reverie and saw what he held in his hand. It was a magnificent stare sapphire, a heavenly blue all around with a radiating white star within. I knew at once that this was to be the gift for my beloved. I purchased it with all the money left in my pockets and returned to my ship. The hyena and tiger were stilled and what remained of the bulging eye of the goat was the star sapphire in my pocket.

So ended my seafaring voyages and my third adventure into the meaning of love.

VI

When the "Victory" had completed its circumambulation of the globe, I found myself where I had begun. I was in excellent spirits and was glad to say a fond farewell to my companions, the good tiger, the dogs and cats and hyenas. The weasel was non-committal, as was the lion — for they had little to do with me — but even the vulture gave me a grudging pat on the back.

With great joy I returned to my ancestral home, laden with gifts for my friends and family. I was greeted with warmth and pleasure by all, who were full of curiosity about my experiences. I told them as best I could, though my words came only with difficulty, for I was thinking always of my beloved. My queries about her were met with an uncomfortable silence all around. At last, I demanded to know where she was, and they told me. She was living, still, in the same city, and I excitedly set out to see her and present her with the treasured star sapphire from India.

When I arrived, I was trembling as I had when I first set eyes upon her, and this was in no way relieved when she opened the door to me. No longer was she veiled; now she was a glorious free woman of beautiful countenance and graceful figure. I let her speak no word, but quickly took her off to the oasis where our love was experienced. She was unquestionably overjoyed to see me, yet I felt her reluctance to join me. I thought that this, indeed, was the remnant of that fateful night that had sent me out into the world and I was sure that when she heard my story, all resistance would vanish.

It was so. As I told her of my adventures and conflicts, her eyes widened, and she listened compassionately. When I told her of the goat, and of my struggles therewith, she sighed deeply. When I told her of the sapphire, and showed it to her, and spoke of my love — she began to weep. She wept and wept for a long time, and I did not understand. Finally she stopped her weeping, embraced me, and told me, haltingly, her story. I will not repeat it in her words, as I was too stunned to take it all in, but, in brief, it was as follows:

That fateful night, when I had raped her, she was indeed darkened. The light had gone out of her eyes, not because of my lust and desire, which she welcomed, but because of my lack of love. Here I nodded sorrowfully. She did not blame me for this deficiency, however, but she blamed herself for her incapacity to evoke love. This statement astonished me so much that she had to repeat it several times. She blamed herself for her incapacity to evoke love in me! In despair, she received the message from my friend that I was going away, presumably forever, and was utterly disconsolate. My friend was kind to her, befriended her, and in truth, fell in love with her. My beloved was healed thereby and gradually grew to love my friend. Shortly before my return, they were married and were very happy together.

This news shocked me. Many feelings passed through me: hurt, anger, despair. We sat silently for a long time, and then I knew what I had to do. "Let this ring be a token of our love, a love that was meant to teach us to love. I love you, and will love you always."

She looked up and accepted the ring, as I carefully placed it on her finger. I embraced her and chanced to look up into the heavens. There, in the crisp night air, hovered a marvelous crescent moon, its curved edges glistening, within a shining star of Venus. I knew that that symbol of my people was also my own, and that it was a living symbol of my capacity to love.

Then my beloved and I made love — and we were happy.

We returned to the city in peaceful joy.

In the days that followed, I had time to reflect upon what I had experienced, and what Allah had set in my path. I became aware that what had really interrupted me in my studies was a realization in the depths of my being, but unavailable to my consciousness, that I was insufficiently capable of love, and that I could never become a healer without this capacity. The experience of my beloved, and all the adventures as a consequence of it, were absolutely necessary for me to enhance this capacity. I now felt right about becoming a healer, and soon resumed my studies. My education for love was further advanced when I saw my betrothed. She, indeed, had loved me deeply, and I did not know it. She had waited patiently for me, and now my love, in truth, began to flow freely to her. We grew closer and closer, loved more deeply. In time, I married, in love; in time, I became a healer, in love; in time, with my beloved, I became a friend, in love.

So ended my fourth adventure into the meaning of love, and so ends my tale.

Thus it is, O Knight, that I meet you here in your garden, which is also my garden. Each of us had his Eden, and here we meet. Come and embrace me, O Knight, as I embrace you, in brotherly love and friendship! Look, there above us, our ancestors, Jacob and Esau, are also embracing, in the Tree of Immortality! Look there, in the heavens, and on the Tree, do you not see it? There I see my crescent moon with its star, and I see that my star and your star are one! Let it be so, O My Brother, let it be so in heaven and on earth, that men are brothers and as one!